CONSPIRACY

Who's Pulling the Strings

CONSPIRACY

World Ahead Press is a division of WND Books. The views and opinions expressed in this book are those of the author and do not necessarily reflect the official policy or position or WND Books.

Hardcover ISBN: 978-1-944212-04-9
eBook ISBN: 978-1-944212-05-6

Printed in the United States of America
16 17 18 19 20 21 XXX 9 8 7 6 5 4 3 2 1

FOREWORD

The writing of a book like this one requires more basic research than I believe is possible for any one mortal human being. While there is a considerable amount of original material in this book, much of the research has been done by others. I have drawn upon the efforts of many authors who have written books on different aspects of the conspiracy. I am including a bibliography of some of these books.

This Conspiracy can be compared to a jigsaw puzzle. When you open the puzzle box and dump out its contents on the table all you see is a lot of little pieces, but when you finally put all the pieces together you usually have a beautiful picture. I have tried to put all the pieces together. To my knowledge there is no other book until now that does that.

I want to warn you though, when we get done we will not have a beautiful picture.

I owe a deep debt of gratitude to each of these authors who put hundreds of hours of research into each piece of the puzzle about which they wrote. I could not have written this book without them.

I also want to acknowledge my own inadequacy. I look to God for His wisdom, understanding, and guidance.

2 Corinthians 12:9 And he said unto me, My grace is sufficient for thee: for my strength is made perfect in weakness. Most gladly therefore will I rather glory in my infirmities, that the power of Christ may rest upon me.

Philippians 4:13 I can do all things through Christ who strengthens me.

INTRODUCTION

My dictionary gives as a definition of conspiracy, "The planning of two or more persons to do an evil act; also, the plan so made." Conspiracy, however, is a word that is very seldom used. When anyone uses the word "conspiracy" the people who hear usually are inclined to add the word "Nut."

Why is this? Have there not been thousands, no millions of times through the centuries when people got together to rob or kill other people for gain? Have there not been conspirators who came together to overthrow governments and do all kinds of evil things? Of course there have. Then why has the word conspiracy gotten such a bad reputation today?

Could it be that those who are involved don't want their conspiratorial ideas exposed? What better way to hide what they are involved in than to call anyone who would try to expose them a "Nut?"

Who are these people who accuse other people of being "Conspiracy Nuts?" They are politicians and the media, (radio, TV, newspapers). The reason they do this is because they are a part of the conspiracy. There are, in fact tens of thousands of people in America today who are a part of the conspiracy and most of them don't even know it. This conspiracy is so huge and so intertwined that only a few are able to see the whole picture. Most people involved only see the objectives that their group is concerned with and have no idea that they are a part of a much larger conspiracy with someone else pulling the strings.

Who is the one pulling the strings? Who is the head of this conspiracy? His name used to be called "Lucifer," which means the "light bearer." Now he is usually referred to as the "Devil" or "Satan".

When we look at the world scene, we see many different groups that seem to be pulling in different directions. There are Socialists, Fascists, One-Worlders, New Agers, Environmentalists, Homosexuals, Educators, Religious Humanists, International Bankers, and many other groups that Satan uses to put together his conspiracy. At first glance, these different groups don't seem to have anything to do with each other, but as we shall see they are all a part of the master plan of Satan.

What is this conspiracy? What is he trying to do? Destroy mankind! That is what he is trying to do. The truth is he hates us. When God first made Adam and Eve in His own image, Satan hated them because he hated God. Indeed Satan would hate any being that resembled God.

Ever since the human race came upon the earth Satan has been trying to destroy them. Satan has plans for you and your children and they are not plans for your wellbeing. One of the main reasons for this book is to expose Satan's plans for our destruction and show how he can be defeated.

The second reason for writing this book is to remind all of us that God also has a plan. Satan wants to destroy us but God wants the best for us. Satan's power is limited but God is Almighty. Satan's plans for our destruction have always failed and they will again.

A reminder to those who live in the United States, God has lifted up America above all other nations, not because of the intelligence of its people, its natural resources or its free enterprise system, but because America's founders dedicated this land to God and because of Christians who have continued to call upon Him.

CONTENTS

ONE

AMERICA TODAY

ECONOMIC AND POLITICAL

Welcome to the information age. The computer is a wonderful tool. No, I would not like to trade my word processor for a typewriter. It is a wonderful thing to be able to go the Internet, type a word in search and almost instantly receive the answer to my quest. Yet, I would gladly trade all the advantages of the information age for the standard of living and freedom we enjoyed 65 years ago. Many of you who are reading this have no memory of this because you weren't born yet. I have the advantage of having lived through those years.

In order to gain perspective on where we are today, let's do a little comparison. When I graduated from High School in 1950, the minimum wage had just been increased to 75 cents an hour. You could buy a loaf of bread for 12 cents and a first class postage stamp for 3 cents. You could rent an apartment for $35 a month, or a home from $45 to $60 a month. If you translate that in today's money you realize that a dollar today only buys what about 6 cents would then. That means that a 75-cent per hour minimum wage in 1950 would be equal to about $12.00 today. Real wages adjusted for inflation have not gone up since 1966. The standard of living for the average worker has actually declined.

The main reason that it takes many more dollars to purchase the same goods today is because we no longer have a monetary system based upon the value of gold and silver. In 1913, contrary to the Constitution of the United States, Congress passed a law which created the Federal Reserve System. We now have a debt-based monetary system which requires the U.S. Treasury to continuously print money to replace the money taken out of the system by interest payments to the bankers who own the Federal Reserve. When new money is printed and comes into the economy, the total amount of money in the system increases but the amount of goods to be purchased does not. It's like pouring water into milk. The volume of liquid increases but the nutritional value does not. The same thing happens to money. When the volume of money increases, but the supply of goods and services stays the same, the value of the money decreases. In other words it becomes worth less until it is worthless. By the end of President George W. Bush's term in office, it took a dollar to buy what 2 cents would have purchased in 1913, when the Federal Reserve was introduced. Since Obama has become President the total money supply has increased 136% in the first 27 months. This will soon result in runaway inflation.

In the 1950s it was customary for the husband and father to work and for the wife and mother to stay home and care for the family. Yes, some women were employed. Some young ladies became nurses, teachers, secretaries, and some of them worked in industry, but it was generally recognized that the most important job was the care of their families. Day Care

Centers for children were almost unheard of. While, "Aid to Dependent Children" or ADC was started in 1935 through the Social Security Act, most unwed mothers either had their children adopted or they received help from their family to raise their child. Divorce was rare.

There were exceptions, of course but generally women went into the work place either before their children were born or after they were much older. Wives usually worked, not out of necessity but in order to buy things like a TV, (which was expensive at that time), or in order to help put the children through college.

Today women have to work just to be able to pay the rent and put food on the table. Is this progress?

While the United States is still the richest country in the world many people find that they are not living near as well as people did many years ago. According to a study done about 18 years ago by the Center on Budget and Policy Priorities, during the previous 22 years the income for the poorest 20% went down 10% in terms of what their money would actually buy. The middle class only rose about 8% even though most of them had become two-wage-earner households. The after-tax income of the top 20% grew by 43% and America's wealthiest 1% increased by 115%. The rich are getting richer while the poor are getting poorer.

Since then the rich are getting much richer, the poor are increasing greatly and the middle class is beginning to disappear.

If our present means of production are more efficient today than they were then, and they are, why are the wages less? Could it be that this is no accident? Could it be that things have been planned to happen this way in order to satisfy the selfish ambitions of greedy bankers and political leaders who have become the unwitting dupes of the master conspirator, Satan?

Please don't misunderstand. I do not wish to indicate that any of our political leaders are smart enough to have figured out the unintended consequences of their selfish actions, but it is still true that actions have consequences, some of which are unintended.

SOCIAL, EDUCATIONAL, MORAL AND SPIRITUAL

If a person who was living a hundred years ago were suddenly transported from the past to today, what do you think would most impress him? At first he would no doubt be impressed with all the wonderful inventions and technology. The automobiles would amaze him and the airplanes even more so. He would be fascinated with radios, TV's, and household appliances. He would no doubt find it almost impossible to believe the things that computers can do.

Some things however, I believe would dismay him. The breakdown of society, the destruction of the family, the perverted education of the children, political correctness, the loss of freedom, and the amount of unbelief in our churches would confuse and dismay him. I believe he would quickly decide that he wanted to go back where he had come from.

We are also dismayed. Why can't Johnny read? Why is it that no matter how much money the schools get, they can't seem to educate our children? Why is it that our children seem to have so little understanding of history? Why are they being trained in a world view that has so little appreciation for the freedoms for which our forefathers bled and died?

Why are our cities in turmoil? Why is there so much racial unrest? Why are there so many poor and poverty stricken people? Why so many unwed mothers? Why so much promiscuity and immorality? Why so much crime?

What has happened to the thinking of the people of the United States? The life of a baby whale is so important that TV networks allot vast amounts of very expensive airtime for it on network news. No mention however, is made of the destruction of millions of babies destroyed in the womb every year. What is happening to our country when we see demonstrations in our streets for homosexual rights, feminists rights, abortion rights, while churches are having a tougher and tougher time even finding a place to build a church building? In many places, town boards are trying to zone them out of existence.

What does it mean when a school tries to keep a child from praying, handing out tracts, or telling others about Jesus on school property, while at the same time the school is teaching religious humanism, witchcraft and New Age religions and now even Islam in their classrooms?

When we see all these things happening we ask: "Are all these things happening by chance or is there a design?" The answer is; these things are happening because they were designed to happen that way. The people who are taking part in these activities usually have no idea that they are taking part in the grand design of the one who is pulling the strings. They are just out for number one - themselves.

THE FAMILY

The family is a microcosm of society. Whatever affects the family will eventually affect all of society.

Many factors affected the family and society in the 20th century. Some of them were due to the industrial revolution, the growth of cities, new technologies etc., but other factors in the breakup of the family were part of a deliberate scheme for world dominion. First let us look at what we might call normal factors.

At the beginning of the twentieth century most families still lived on farms. There were a few steam tractors, but most of the tilling of the soil was done by horse or mule power. The children were expected to do their part in bringing in the crops. When the children were not in school they spent most of their time with their parents who trained and disciplined them in the way they should go. The grandparents usually lived with the family and the children also received their wisdom.

THE DESTRUCTION OF THE FAMILY

As farming became more efficient and manufacturing increased, many children who had been raised on the farm moved to the city. This caused a decrease in the extended family. Fathers who worked in the factories came home tired and did not have as much contact with their children. Children in the city had more free time. When they came home from school they did not have to go to the fields instead their chores were now helping to cook, clean, wash dishes, carry out the trash, etc. Because children had more time on their hands schools began to provide more activities to help keep them out of trouble.

Wives and mothers also had more time to pursue the things outside the home. While husbands were often distracted by other women with whom they came in contact at work or in a bar where they might stop off for a beer before going home. All of these things contributed to the destruction of the family, but there was no design or intention to do so. We might consider all of these things as normal factors of a changed society.

THE INTENTIONAL DESTRUCTION OF THE FAMILY

Some things were deliberately designed to destroy the family. They were planned and executed for that very purpose.

Does that statement seem unbelievable to you? Why would anyone in their right mind want to destroy the family and thereby destroy civilization? The answer is power, money and control.

Every totalitarian power has undermined the family in order to increase their total control. Hitler organized the brown shirts for German children. They were taught to spy on and betray their parents. The communists of Russia followed the same pattern.

In his book "1984" George Orwell described how Big Brother was the all-important one. He came before any family member and he had his agents always watching people. They used TV cameras to see if people might be committing thought crimes. Aldous Huxley in his book, "Brave New World" describes a world order in which not only the family but even sex is destroyed so that the rulers might have complete control.

Considering these things should it really come as a complete surprise that those who have been planning for a New World Order would not also plan for the destruction of the family so that they would be able to take control? They considered it a necessity to destroy the family because it is in the family setting that values and traditions are passed on.

The New World Order seeks to replace all the old values and traditions with their own agenda.

First they needed to get rid of the father and the intact family. "Aid to Dependant Children" has served in this capacity quite nicely

"Aid to Dependent Children" is responsible for more social unrest and destruction than anything else I can think of. In the following paragraphs I intend to illustrate how "Aid to Dependent Children" has destroyed the family, produced more children without a father and made all of us poorer.

When "Aid to Dependent Children" was being discussed the lawmakers didn't want dead-beat dads to be taking advantage of any of this money. Therefore they made a rule that they would not subsidize a family if an able bodied man who was the father of the children was residing in the home. The result was that if a man lost his job and either couldn't find work or had to settle for a job at half the pay, he had a problem. If he stayed in the home and helped raise the children, the family would be ineligible to receive help under this program. The only way that his family could receive food and shelter from this program would require him to move out.

In many cases the men moved out. However, if another man moved in, they would be able to continue to receive help because he was not the father of the children. This rule perhaps more than anything else is responsible for large numbers of fatherless children. It has wrecked havoc in the black community and is increasingly doing so also in the white community.

The congressmen who wrote the law had no idea that they were following Satan's plan. They were simply trying to look out for their own interests. If they had really wanted to help the children, they would have assisted the whole family sufficiently to help them get over the crisis. Then the family could have been preserved and all of society would have benefited.

Unfortunately that was not their real goal. What they really wanted to do was to get re-elected. Therefore, they doled out just enough money to help people get by but never enough for them to get back on their feet. That way they would be forever dependent and continue to vote for the people that gave them the money.

"Aid to Dependent Children" also had a number of other consequences. It increased the number of illegitimate children because with only one child a mother would have to work; but if she had three, four, or five, she could live well without working.

It took away the responsibility of being a husband and father from young men. After all, the government would take care of them. This kind of thinking probably wasn't prevalent for the first welfare generation, but it certainly was for the second and third generation.

It is also responsible for filling up prisons. If you check out the prison system, you will find that most of the inmates come from broken and dysfunctional homes.

This law, instead of helping the children has destroyed the family. The children have been greatly harmed because they have had to grow up without the guidance and role model of a good father.

Of course "Aid to Dependent Children" is not all bad. It has helped to provide food, clothing and shelter to hundreds of thousands of mothers and children, which was very much needed. The question remains. Is this the best way to help families? I think not. This law has not only wasted money on welfare spending, but also by the need to increase spending for prisons, crime, the breakup of the family and social unrest.

While "Aid to Dependent Children" worked very well to destroy the families of the poor, something else was needed for the more affluent families.

"The Mind, (we are told) is a terrible thing to waste." Rest assured, the Globalists do not intend to waste any opportunity to influence it for their agenda. They know full well that in order to set up a New World Order national governments must lose their power and influence, and that in order to establish a World Religion the present religion of Christians, Jews and Muslims must be molded into one. How can this be accomplished? The answer is by education of course. Actually education is really the wrong word. It should really be called brainwashing.

EDUCATIONAL BRAINWASHING

The brainwashing of young impressionable minds starts very early. The children are eager to understand and learn about life. After parents, teachers are their main sources of knowledge. It is well known and understood that character and attitudes about life are formed very early in the life of a child. In order to reach the child it is first necessary to prepare and train the teacher and to do that you have to start at the top with the University professors.

The professors trained the teachers who gradually replaced the older teachers and the old teaching material.

Since the 1930's several generations of teachers have come and gone. The result is that a whole generation has graduated from high school that can barely read and write. These high school graduates have very little knowledge of history, geography, constitutional government, or economics but they are extremely self confident. They think they are very smart because they know more about computers than their parents do.

In the Introduction to Brave New World, Aldous Huxley wrote, "A really efficient totalitarian state would be one in which the all powerful executive of political bosses and their army of managers control a population of slaves who do not have to be coerced, because they love their servitude, To make them love it is the task assigned, in present day totalitarian states, to ministries of propaganda, newspaper editors and schoolteachers."

So, what are the children in our public schools learning? Perhaps we should first ask, "What they are not learning." They are not learning to read very well. They are not learning to speak good English or write it. They are not learning U.S. History, Geography, or Constitutional Government. In a recent survey of High School students all over the world U.S. High School Seniors ranked near the bottom in Science and Math. Even though the seniors ranked near the bottom they felt very good about themselves. Evidently knowledge is not considered very important for today's students. It's how they think and feel about themselves that is most important.

They are also not learning to be proud of their country. They are not learning the true reasons why the colonists braved tremendous hardship to come and make a new life in America. They are not being taught that the foundations of this nation, the Constitution of the United States and the Bill of Rights were based on the Bible. They are not taught that Constitutional Law and Common Law of England were based on the Bible. They are not taught that the freedoms found in America are Bible based. They are not learning about true American heroes nor are they learning to feel proud to be an American.

What then are they learning? They are learning to feel good about themselves but question the motives and ideas of their parents and ministers of the Gospel. They are learning about sex and homosexuality. They are learning to question their own sexuality. They are learning that there is no absolute right or wrong. Boys are being taught to be more like girls and girls are being taught to be like boys.

What is this kind of education all about? It's all very simple. If you want to establish a "New World Order" with "One World Government" you first have to get rid of patriotism and nationalism. That's why the schools no longer teach the quotation of Patrick Henry, "Give me liberty, or give me death". They do not want to teach the children to become citizens of the United States but citizens of the World. The educational establishment does not want the children to learn the true facts about the history of this country. Instead they are given just enough facts which have been slanted the right way so that Dick and Jane will think the way they are programmed.

Dr. Paul Vitz, a professor of psychology at New York University, headed a panel which examined about 60 history and social study textbooks used in the nation's public schools. What they found was shocking. Almost all Christian history had been removed from the textbooks. In the first four grades they did not find any mention of Christianity and in a fifth grade book "Fundamentalists" were described as people who followed ancient agricultural ways. Pilgrims were defined as people who took long trips. There was virtually no mention of the beliefs of the Founding Fathers and no positive reference to the Christian faith, which formed the bedrock foundation of our republican form of government.

To further come against Christianity and Biblical morality they teach that there is no right or wrong. Sex education is being taught, not for the purpose of warning against the dangers of promiscuity or disease, but teaching them how to do it. Then if they get into trouble, there is always abortion.

Intimacy games are introduced to get the children over their inhibitions against touching one another. While supposedly trying to combat discrimination and judgmentalism, the schools have pushed a pro-homosexual agenda. They started doing this with the older children but now they are even going after the preschoolers. In 1997 the school board of Provincetown, Massachusetts, voted to begin educating preschoolers about homosexuality.

To further breakdown the Christian foundation Indian and Eastern religions have been introduced to the children. By the middle of the 1980s, horoscopes, séances, witches, and Ouija boards also flooded the classrooms. Witches and neo-pagans were invited to speak in public schools where Christian ministers were forbidden.

In the name of discovering their life purpose children are encouraged to go into trance-like states of mind where they communicate with guardian spirits. Yoga and other mind control techniques are also used to help the children contact their inner wisdom and higher selves.

How successful have they been? In 1992, The Barna Group conducted a survey which asked about fundamental beliefs by Americans. Sixty six percent of American adults believed that "there is no such thing as absolute truth" and that "different people can define truth in conflicting ways and still be correct". In the 18 to 25 year old group, 72 percent gave this response.

I know that there are many fine Christian teachers who are doing the best job they know how with the materials they have to work with. The problem is the NEA (National Educational Association), the school administrators, and the courts have tied their hands as to what they are able to teach. For many teachers that is not a problem. They have already been brainwashed. This redirection of our educational system wasn't done overnight. It started with John Dewey in the 1930s. He is said to be the father of American progressive education. He considered behavior-shaping the highest educational objective. Now the old morals and ethics could be replaced by situational ethics or values clarification. Reading, writing, and arithmetic were not considered near as important as sensitivity training and self esteem. A recent survey of 17 year olds revealed that a majority could not place the Civil War in the correct fifty-year span, nor could they locate the state of New York on a map. They did not know what event brought the U.S. into World War II. As a result we now have a whole generation of functional, cultural, and moral illiterates.

John Dewey was a Fabian Socialist. Fabian Socialism started in England within a year after the death of Karl Marx. John Dewey was one of the first of the elite in America to embrace their beliefs and sign the Humanist Manifesto. Unlike Marxist Communists Fabian Socialists did not advocate a violent overthrow of governments. Instead, they opted for a more gradual approach. They wished to accomplish the same thing by gradually influencing and taking over in the fields of literature, politics, education, science and the media. They started in the universities where they trained the teachers, the lawyers, the scientists, and the journalists.

Another big name in the breakdown of the family and American society is Margaret Sanger. She was the founder of Planned Parenthood. She advocated unrestrained sexuality especially among teenagers, but once they started doing what she advocated, her solution was sterilization and abortion. In 1920 she published a book called "Breeding the Thoroughbred". In it she called for building a master race through eugenics or good genes. She declared that only way to do that was to cull out all undesirable people through involuntary sterilization. Sex was promoted as the means to accomplish her purpose. Unrestrained sex meant unwanted pregnancies. The solution to the problem of unwanted babies was sterilization and abortion.

She wanted to sterilize blacks, Jews, southern Europeans, fundamentalist Christians, mentally impaired, and the relatives of the mentally impaired. The Rockefeller and Ford Foundations heavily funded her. Parts of her program of sterilization of the mentally defective was considered by the Indiana Legislature and made part of Indiana law. Adolph Hitler later used the Indiana model for his program to eliminate the unfit.

THE ROLE OF THE SUPREME COURT

The conspirators have realized that in order to get the American people to accept a socialistic all-powerful government at the expense of their freedom; and to eventually be ready to accept a world government, it would be necessary to destroy the

Christian consensus. They also realized that no elected body would pass their radical agenda. So they found a way around the legislatures. They would accomplish their purposes through the judicial system. For a long time they have tried to make sure that only liberal, left leaning judges would be appointed. They zeroed in on all Federal judgeships, but especially the Supreme Court.

When any judge they don't like is nominated they mount a smear campaign, hold hearings, won't bring them up for a vote, and threaten a filibuster.

They borked Judge Bork. They smeared Clarence Thomas and they wouldn't bring any of George W. Bush's nominees up for a vote.

It really doesn't matter what the qualification of the nominees are. The only thing these conspirators are concerned about is their social agenda. What they want to do is rewrite the Constitution, not through the ballot but through judicial decisions. A former Harvard law professor Felix Frankfurter, who became a Supreme Court Justice, is said to have passed a note to another Justice which read, "If we can keep old bushy (another Supreme Court Justice) on our side, there's no amount of rewriting the constitution that we can't do".

So, how much success have they had in destroying America's Christian foundation? In 1947 the Supreme Court invented the doctrine of "separation of church and state".

In 1958 the Supreme Court announced that they were the "supreme law of the land". Of course that was unconstitutional, but to my knowledge, no one ever challenged them. Without a challenge, that gave the Court the right to make up the constitution as it goes along.

On June 25, 1962, the Supreme Court ruled that prayer could not be said in the public schools. On June 17, 1963, they ruled that the Bible could not be read in the classroom. In 1973, the Supreme Court voted to allow babies to be ripped out of their mother's womb through abortion. In 1980, the Court ruled that the Ten Commandments could not be posted in the classroom. In 1984, they ruled that even a moment of silence at the beginning of classes was unconstitutional if it was used for silent prayer.

THE FOLLOWING IS FROM THE "WORLDNETDAILY.COM WEBSITE:

- In Texas, a U.S. District judge decreed that any student uttering the word "Jesus" at his school's graduation would be arrested and locked up. "And make no mistake;" announced Judge Samuel B. Kent, "the court is going to have a United States marshal in attendance at the graduation. If any student offends this court, that student will be summarily arrested and will face up to six months incarceration in the Galveston County Jail for contempt of court."

- In Missouri, when fourth-grader Raymond Raines bowed his head in prayer before his lunch in the cafeteria of Waring Elementary School in St. Louis, his teacher allegedly ordered him out of his seat, in full view of other students present, and sent him to the principal's office. After his third such prayer "offense," little Raymond was segregated from his classmates, ridiculed for his religious beliefs, and given one week's detention.

- In New York, kindergartner Kayla Broadus recited the familiar and beloved prayer – "God is great, God is good. Thank you, God, for my food" – while holding hands with two students seated next to her at her snack table at her Saratoga Springs school early last year. But she was silenced and scolded by her teacher, who reported the infraction to the school's lawyer, Gregg T. Johnson, who concluded that Kayla's behavior was indeed a violation of the "separation of church and state."

  "Separation of church and state" was used by the ACLU to demand that a banner proclaiming "God bless America," erected outside a school shortly after Sept. 11, 2001, to honor the 3,000 murdered Americans, must be taken down.

  "Separation of church and state" was used to deny a little, handicapped girl the right to read her Bible on the bus on the long trip to school.

  "Separation of church and state" was used to take Justice Roy Moore's 10 Commandments monument out of the Alabama Judicial Building, and it is being used right now to challenge the words "under God" in the Pledge of Allegiance.

The phrase "separation of church and state" is not found in the First Amendment of the Constitution or in any the writings of our Founding Fathers.

While all this was happening, where were the shepherds? Where were the church leaders, the pronouncements by church conventions, and letters to congress? Why did the churches take all this like a dog that is afraid to bark?

No doubt some in the churches would quote Romans 13:1 "Let every soul be subject unto the higher powers. For there is no power but of God: the powers that be are ordained of God".

In America it should be remembered that we are the government. Is not the government of the United States "of the people, by the people, and for the people"? If all those who call themselves Christian were to stand together for the things that are right, what politician could stand against them? The problem is that not all who call themselves Christian really are.

Of those pastors and churches that claim to believe the Bible, why are most of them also silent? For some it is the case of feeling helpless, but for others it is a case of abandonment theology as John W. Chalfant describes it in his book called "Abandonment Theology". He says that Christians are losing America because when they observed what was happening in America, they decided that we must be living in the last days. Therefore the "rapture of the church" is near, so why fight it. "After all," these clergymen said, "We're in this world, not of it, so to heck with it," and "Compared to eternity we're here only for an instant." They told us that all that really counts is that we "lead as many people as possible to salvation and let our corrupted country continue on its death course."

With that kind of attitude, America's destruction is assured. John Chalfant goes on to describe the decline of Judeo-Christian influence in law, culture and public policy after the 1947 Supreme Court decision that invented the modern doctrine of "separation of church and state." He writes: "Once God was shown the door, America went into chaos. Scholastic Aptitude Test scores plummeted. Violent crime rocketed upward. The abortion mills did an unprecedented business as they devised ever-more-sadistic ways to kill children before and even during birth. Bill Clinton, elected president of the United States in 1992, aggressively advocated homosexuality, which God calls 'an abomination.' The Abandonment Clergy and their millions of undiscerning followers stood mute while America's sudden loss of greatness became obvious even to the world."

SOMETHING TO KEEP IN MIND

You might have noticed that the words socialist, left leaning and conspirators are almost interchangeable. If we think of the Conspiracy in terms of political parties, then the extreme left of the Democratic Party pretty well fits that definition. I have tried to steer clear of political parties because it is not that simple. The fact is that there are members of both political parties who are part of the Conspiracy. In fact every president of the United States, with the exception of Ronald Reagan, from Franklin D. Roosevelt until now has been part of the Conspiracy.

THE ROLE OF THE MEDIA

Without a doubt the media (radio, TV, and the printed word) play one of the most powerful roles in the Conspiracy. They have been trained well for their roles by socialistic, left leaning teachers; and they are being directed by leftist organizations to which they belong.

Members of the Conspiracy have bought practically all the major news media. This includes CBS, NBC, ABC, CNBC, all the major newspapers and all the major news magazines and almost all the Hollywood movie studios.

If you were to ask the average journalist; "Are you a part of the Conspiracy?" They would look at you like you were crazy. "What conspiracy?" they might reply. "I am just reporting the news as I see it". I am sure that most journalists have no idea that they are part of any kind of conspiracy.

They are just doing what they have been trained to do. They write the way they do because that is the way they have been taught to believe is right, but they work under the direction of editors and owners who know and push the New World Order.

So what do these journalists do that is so bad? They push the leftist agenda every chance they get. If for instance they are reporting on President Clinton's sexual indiscretion they make light of it. If on the other hand they were reporting any hint of scandal in Ronald Reagan's administration they talk about the grave consequences of such activity. If a bill comes before Congress that would cut taxes they proclaim dire warnings about such reckless action and furthermore point out how it will hurt the widows and orphans as well as cause grandmothers to have to eat dog food. On the other hand if a spending and welfare bill comes before Congress they play up all the great benefits of this humanitarian gesture. By their words and emphases they try to sway the listener or reader to the leftist viewpoint. They don't stop there though. They do far worse things.

They report truth selectively. When reporting a news event they spend a great deal of time reporting the things which are favorable to their point of view but skip quickly over those things which are unfavorable. If there is a panel discussion of events on TV, they pack the panel. They will place one conservative on a panel with five or six liberals.

When the conservative finally gets a chance to speak the liberals on the panel will talk over him so that you can't hear what he has to say.

Hollywood and TV sitcoms have their own way of pushing the leftist agenda. In the 1950's TV featured programs like the Nelson's, Leave it to Beaver and My Three Sons. These programs were perhaps a little too idealistic but they featured wholesome families with the father pictured as wise and in control. Today the TV fare has completely changed. If there is a father in the home he is pictured as an incompetent boob who just makes a lot of noise. Ministers of the Gospel are usually portrayed as immoral, money grubbing or irrelevant.

Somewhere I read that if you want to set up a people group for destruction first you portray them as a non-person. You make them into a stereotype that must be destroyed. The Germans used this method to portray the Jews as grotesque, money-grubbing and immoral. All the troubles that the German people had experienced were blamed on the Jews. During World War II the Japanese were portrayed in cartoons as grotesque. Is it too much to think that one-day Bible believing Christians might be portrayed as intolerant, mean-spirited, homophobic wife beaters and child abusers?

The media has succeeded very well in executing their leftist agenda. When the major newspapers, the magazines, and TV news all proclaim the same message the public usually accepts it. The good news is that there are now some conservative radio and TV hosts that are now proclaiming the truth. The truth can be found but you must search for it. Unfortunately most people have neither the time nor the inclination to do the searching.

OTHER CONSPIRACY PLAYERS

Some of the other conspiracy players are: New Agers, Environmentalists, Feminists, Gun Banners, Atheistic Humanists, and Christian Apostates. Whole books can and have been written on each of these subjects. It is not the purpose of this book to repeat all the information in these books, but to try to help you to see the whole picture. There is a saying, "He can't see the forest for the trees." What that means is that if you are too close to something you can only see a part of it. If you want to see the forest you need to get out of the trees and perhaps into an airplane high above the forest. Only then can you see how vast the forest really is. For that reason I am only going to write a short paragraph on each subject so that we can move on to see the whole picture.

New Agers' beliefs vary but they generally follow the pattern of religions of the Far East. Some of them worship Gaia (mother earth). Some are pantheistic (the belief that everything is a part of God). They do not believe that Christ as an actual person. When they speak of Christ in you they are not talking about Jesus but rather the acknowledgement of the god within you. Others are looking for a new age cosmic Christ who would be a reincarnation of the great holy men of past ages. They are looking for this cosmic Christ that they refer to as Lord Maitreya to bring the people of earth into a utopian dream society. The New Agers are greatly influencing society especially in the schools, medicine, politics and the environment. They have also made great inroads in the churches.

Environmentalists base their beliefs and actions mostly on false science. Most true scientists do not agree with them but those who do are very vocal. Every true Christian should be concerned about the environment because God put man in charge to take care of it. However, that is the exact opposite of what the environmentalists want. They see man as a virus upon planet earth. Man needs to be eliminated or at least his numbers greatly reduced so that earth can be restored to its pristine state. The educators go alone with this because it fits in with their philosophy. Many politicians go along because it fits in with their ambitions for power and land grabs. The media plays along because it furthers the one world agenda. Logic, reason, and facts are unimportant when talking to an environmentalist; because to him it is a matter of faith. It is his religion.

Feminists in their supposed quest for equality with men are denying women of all the protections and sense of worth that makes being a woman something special. They have tried to convince women that the only thing that is important is to have a career and make money. They try to deny a woman the joy of motherhood and the satisfaction of raising her children to become productive citizens.

The Gun Banners want to get rid of all guns that a person could use for self-defense. It has been well said, "When guns are outlawed only the out-laws will have guns." I know that there are some people who sincerely believe that the world would be a much safer place without guns. Actually the facts do not bear this out. In fact the very opposite is true. In those states and cities with the most restrictive gun legislation the crime rate and murder is the highest. Switzerland is a country that hasn't been in a war or invaded by a hostile power for a long, long time. They have a law that every household must possess a reliable weapon and know how to use it. No country has dared to invade Switzerland because they know every citizen is a soldier.

Think about it. If you were a crook which home would you rather break in, one where the owner might have a gun or one that you know the guns have been removed from? But, what do facts and logic have to do with it?

The first thing every would be dictator, tries to do is to first register the guns and then pick them up. Without weapons the citizens cannot fight back.

Atheistic Humanists have been trying to undermine Christianity and set up a secular state. The Humanist Manifesto which was first published in 1933 states that man is just a part of nature and that it is time for religion to be done away with. Humanists are to be found just about everywhere but are especially exemplified by the ACLU in its constant warfare against any mention of God it the public arena. They, along with the courts, have gotten God out of the public schools. They succeeded in getting the Ten Commandments removed from a courthouse in Alabama. They would also like to get "In God we trust" off of our coins and get God removed from the pledge of allegiance.

Christian Apostates have been undermining the church in America for many years. In a later chapter, we will look at the roots of the apostasy but for now we will just look at the results. In the 1930's G.H. Betts of Northwestern University sent out a survey to 1309 ministers. 500 of them replied. The results: Over half believed in miracles but a third of them denied that miracles were ever performed. Only 87 percent believed that God was all-powerful. Only 48 percent of Congregational ministers believed that God was unchangeable. Those who rejected the doctrine of the Trinity were: Congregational 64 percent, Methodist 28 percent, and Baptist 14 percent. Concerning Creation, less than 47 percent believed the Genesis account. Since then things have continued to get worse.

In 1982 sociologist Jeffery Hadden surveyed 10,000 Protestant pastors and found that a majority of them had lost their faith. Over 45 percent of the pastors did not believe that Jesus Christ is God, 80 percent did not believe that the Bible is the inspired Word of God, and 35 percent did not believe that Jesus Christ rose from the dead.

The people in the pews have also picked up on the unbelief of the pastors. In 1992 The Barna Group conducted a survey which asked about fundamental beliefs by Americans. Sixty six percent of American adults believed that there is no such thing as absolute truth, and that different people can define truth in conflicting ways and still be correct.

In the next chapter we will look at the roots of the Conspiracy and see how it all began.

CHAPTER 2

HOW IT ALL BEGAN

What is this Conspiracy all about? It is about hatred, jealousy, and destruction. It is about the disappointment and ambitions of one of the most beautiful and powerful beings of the universe. Here is how it all began.

From what we read in the Bible, Satan was one of the most beautiful and powerful of the angels God had created. God called this very beautiful angel Lucifer, which means, "light bearer". He was a master musician and full of wisdom. Without a doubt he was a great leader that the other angels looked up to because when he rebelled against God, a third of the angels joined him in the rebellion. Why did he rebel? We don't know for sure but it is quite possible that he rebelled because God had decided to make man. God was going to make man in His own image and breathe into man His spirit. God was also giving man the power and authority to rule over his physical creation on earth. Furthermore, God was now charging the angels to serve man. Perhaps all this was just too much for Lucifer. He was not about to let man take what he thought was his rightful place. Therefore he rebelled.

Why, we might ask, did God want to create man when he already had created such beautiful and marvelous creatures as the angels? I believe the answer is fellowship.

Yes, God had already created the angels and the animals, but it was impossible for God to have full fellowship with them. The angels were marvelous spiritual beings which were created for God's glory, but they did not bear God's nature or image. The animals had marvelous bodies. They had rational minds and emotions, but they were not spiritual beings. They were governed by the instincts with which they were created.

In order for God to have full fellowship with another being, it would have to be with someone like Himself. Neither the angels nor the animals fit that description. That's why I believe He created man. He made them in His own image and likeness.

Now that Satan had rebelled against God, the hatred that he had for God was now directed toward man. If he could not destroy God, perhaps He could destroy God's most prized creation. The question was, how? Man was under God's protection. Not only that, but the whole earth had been put under man's rule and control. There was no way to touch man directly. If man was to be destroyed, he would have to be tricked into rebelling against God so that God would destroy him.

Satan must have been full of glee when God himself seemed to provide the way for man's destruction. God had placed two special trees in the Garden of Eden, the "Tree of Life" and the "Tree of the Knowledge of Good and Evil". Satan knew that God had placed the tree of the Knowledge of Good and Evil in the Garden with the command that man should not eat of it. The purpose was to prove man's loyalty and willing obedience. God had told man the day he ate of it he would surely die. Man had no reason to doubt God's word. God had given man this beautiful world. How could

Satan get man to doubt God? Suddenly the answer came. He would make man envious of God and goad man with the idea that he himself could be like God. Now all he had to do was bide his time.

He decided to try with the woman first. If she could be deceived then she could help lure Adam into the trap. Soon the day arrived. Eve was by herself at the moment. Satan entered the body of a snake and called to Eve. Eve must have thought that the snake was some wonderful creature in order to be able to talk to her, so she came where he was to find out more. Then Satan spoke through the snake. ***"Has God indeed said, 'You shall not eat of every tree of the garden'?"*** ***Gen. 3:1*** Satan knew full well what God's command was; but he was trying to imply that God was unjust, that He was withholding something good from them.

> And the woman said unto the serpent, We may eat of the fruit of the trees of the garden: But of the fruit of the tree which is in the middle of the garden, God has said, You shall not eat of it, neither shall you touch it, lest you die.
>
> GEN 3: 2, 3

The Bible doesn't say whether God told them not to touch it. It would have been sufficient though for Eve to say that they were commanded not to eat of it. When Satan heard her add the words not to touch it, he knew that he had gotten to her. He had only mentioned eating but she had added touching. Now he knew he had her.

> And the serpent said unto the woman, you will not surely die: For God knows that in the day you eat of it, then your eyes will be opened, and you will be like God, knowing good and evil.
>
> GEN 1: 4, 5

What an interesting concept; to be like God. If only we had this knowledge, we could be like God. In fact, if we could be like God, then we wouldn't need God. We could be our own gods. This is the root sin. Every sin is a rebellion against God and an attempt to throw Him off of His throne. This is central to the false teachings of Mormonism that as God was we are and that we can also become like God. This concept is also one of the main delusions of the New Age religion. When they speak of **Christ Consciousness** and **Christ in you**, they are not talking about receiving the Lord Jesus Christ through faith. No, they have instead deluded themselves into thinking they are Christ and that they are a part of God.

Now when Satan tries to deceive Eve into believing that she can be like God, she thought about it. That was a mistake. You cannot defeat Satan by trying to reason with him. He is a very clever and crafty fellow. He has had thousands of years to perfect his craft of deception. The only way to defeat Satan is with the Word of God. When the Holy Spirit led Jesus into the wilderness and He was tempted of the devil. He said, *"It is written."*

Eve could have replied, "God made this whole creation and me also. He said that if I eat of this tree I will die. I have no reason to doubt Him. I will do as He has said." Instead she takes a good look at the fruit and begins to reason with herself.

It looks good and it smells good. God Himself said that it was the tree of the Knowledge of Good and Evil. Isn't knowledge good? Why would God withhold something good? Could it be true? If she ate of it, would she gain this new knowledge and be like God Himself? She picks the fruit; nothing happens. She looks at it carefully and then bites into it. Something happened. She doesn't know what, but it's like the entire world has changed. She knows that she is different, but she doesn't want to be alone. She calls to Adam and when he comes to her, she says," Here Adam, take a bite. See it hasn't hurt me. The snake says it will make us wise and we will be like God."

Instantly he realizes that Eve has been deceived. He loves her. He doesn't want to lose her. Whatever is going to happen, he will share it with her. Without a word, he takes the fruit and eats.

Suddenly their eyes were opened and they knew they were naked. What a great revelation it was! Their first new knowledge was shame. Then when God called to them, they learned another bit of knowledge. They learned what fear was. The Bible says they ran away and tried to hide. What terrible thing had they done? Were they now about to be destroyed? God had said, *"For in the day that you eat of it you shall surely die."*

As a matter fact that is exactly what happened. Oh yes, their hearts were still beating, but they had lost the image of God and they had died spiritually. They were no longer in fellowship with God. They were separated from the source of life, their Creator. The seed of death was now planted and little by little their bodies would begin to loose their vitality. The process of physical death had now begun.

Man had sinned. He had rebelled against God. He no longer loved God because he was afraid of Him. Everything beautiful had now become ugly. Instead of coming to God to fellowship with Him, all they now wanted to do was run away.

Who could have blamed God if he had destroyed them outright? However, God had other plans. Satan had instigated man's sin in order to bring about man's destruction. Nevertheless, God still loved the man and woman whom He had created. In their present condition, they could not come back to Him so He would have to go to them. However, there was a big problem.

Man had sinned. The justice of God demanded payment. In addition, man himself had changed. He no longer loved God but was afraid of Him. Instead of coming to God he was now trying to run away from God as fast as possible. He had to be turned around. Sin had to be paid for. The only suitable payment was death. A man would have to die to make the payment for sin, but Adam and Eve could not make the payment of restoration because they were guilty. An innocent man would have to volunteer to bear the sin of the guilty so that God's justice might be satisfied and so the guilty could be restored. God had a plan. He would send forth His own Son to earth that He might take on human flesh and become a man. Jesus, the Son of God, would voluntarily make payment for sin through His suffering and death on the cross and by His great love, would draw mankind back to God.

> For God so loved the world, that he gave his only begotten Son, that whoever believes in him should not perish, but have everlasting life.
>
> For God sent not his Son into the world to condemn the world; but that the world through him might be saved. He that believes on him is not condemned: but he that does not believe is condemned already, because he has not believed in the name of the only begotten Son of God.
>
> JOHN 3: 16-18

Then God spoke to Adam and Eve. He promised that a male child would be born of a woman sometime in the future who would crush Satan's head.

> And I will put enmity between you and the woman, and between your seed (the children of the Satan) and her Seed; (those who follow Jesus) He shall bruise (or crush) your head, and you shall bruise His heel." (or wound him)
>
> GEN 3:15

This was the first promise of a Savior. The promise was rather vague, but our first parents understood that this child would someday crush Satan's head and thereby restore mankind to favor with God. This promise was to be repeated to Noah, then to Abram, to Moses, to David and to all the prophets. Each prophecy added additional information. All these bits of information began to form a composite picture of the coming Savior. All together about 350 prophecies of the coming Savior was recorded. When Jesus came, people should have been able to recognize Him, but they didn't.

> He was in the world, and the world was made by him, and the world did not know him. He came unto his own, and his own did not receive him. But as many as received him, to them gave he power to become the sons of God, even to them that believe on his name: Which were born, not of blood, nor of the will of the flesh, nor of the will of man, but of God.
>
> And the Word was made flesh, and dwelt among us, (and we beheld his glory, the glory as of the only begotten of the Father,) full of grace and truth.
>
> JOHN 1: 10-14

The amazing thing is that while God wanted mankind to know and understand these prophecies, their meaning was completely hidden from Satan and all his demonic hordes.

> And my speech and my preaching was not with enticing words of man's wisdom, but in demonstration of the Spirit and of power: That your faith should not stand in the wisdom of men, but in the power of God.
>
> Although we speak wisdom among them that are mature: yet not the wisdom of this world, nor of the rulers of this world, who are coming to nothing: But we speak the wisdom of God in a mystery, even the hidden wisdom, which God ordained before the ages for our glory:
>
> Which none of the princes of this world knew: for had they known it, they would not have crucified the Lord of glory.
>
> 1 COR 2: 4-8

What looked like a complete victory for Satan turned out to be very hollow and empty. It was only a partial victory. It is true that man had sinned, but he was not yet destroyed.

Somehow Satan would have to maneuver man into such a wicked state that God would destroy him. Satan didn't have the authority to destroy man himself, but he now possessed an advantage. Since man had sinned once, it would be easier to deceive and tempt mankind again.

I am sure Satan was disappointed that he had been unable to get God to destroy man, but he doesn't give up easily. He would continue again and again in his efforts to destroy man.

CHAPTER 3

ALMOST DESTROYED

And Adam knew Eve his wife; and she conceived, and gave birth to Cain, and said, "I have gotten a man from the LORD." And she again gave birth to his brother Abel. And Abel was a keeper of sheep, but Cain was a tiller of the ground.

And in process of time it came to pass, that Cain brought of the fruit of the ground an offering unto the LORD. And Abel, he also brought of the firstlings of his flock and of the fat portions. And the LORD respected Abel and to his offering: But he did not respect Cain and his offering. And Cain was very angry, and his countenance fell.

And the LORD said unto Cain, Why are you angry? And why is your countenance fallen? If you do well, will you not be accepted? And if you do not well, sin lies at the door. And its desire is for you, but you must rule over it. And Cain talked with Abel his brother: and it came to pass, when they were in the field, that Cain rose up against Abel his brother, and killed him.

GEN 4: 1-8

When Cain was born Eve make a very peculiar statement. She said, "*I have gotten a man from the Lord*" In the original Hebrew the word, "from" is missing. What she actually said was, "I have gotten a man, the Lord." Apparently she was applying the first promise of the coming Savior to Cain. Sadly, she was badly mistaken. After Cain's brother, Abel, was born there seemed to be a rivalry between them. No doubt both of them wanted to excel. Abel was a herdsman and took care of animals while Cain was a farmer. Their rivalry came to a head with the offering of sacrifice to God.

We don't have the specific instructions that God gave Adam and Eve concerning worship and sacrifice. We only know what is recorded in the Bible. We do know however what the Bible says at a later date.

> For when Moses had spoken every precept to all the people according to the law, he took the blood of calves and of goats, with water, and scarlet wool, and hyssop, and sprinkled both the book, and all the people, Saying, This is the blood of the testament which God hath enjoined unto you.
>
> Moreover he sprinkled with blood both the tabernacle, and all the vessels of the ministry. And almost all things are by the law purged with blood; and *without shedding of blood is no remission.*
>
> HEB 9: 19-22

All the sacrifices in the Old Testament looked forward to the coming of Christ, who, as the Lamb of God would shed his blood for the sins of the world. I believe it is safe to conclude that Adam and Eve were also instructed in blood sacrifice.

Adam and Eve would surely have instructed both Cain and Abel. Evidently, Cain was a very proud and stubborn man. Since Cain was a farmer he didn't have any animals to offer. Of course, Cain could have traded some of his produce with Abel for a lamb but he was too proud to do that. He probably thought, "Why isn't my lettuce, cucumbers and melons just as good as a lamb?" So that's what he did. He offered the fruits of his labor as sacrifice. However, this is not what God commanded or was happy with. The Bible at another place says that God desires obedience more than sacrifice. It was not a question of which was more valuable -- the fruits and vegetables or the lamb. It was a question of what was an acceptable offering to God.

When Cain sees that God is not pleased with his offering he becomes angry with his brother, Abel. Now isn't that a strange thing? It was Cain who disobeyed God's command. He should have been angry with himself. Instead, he was jealous of his brother, who had obeyed God and received God's approval. God then reproved Cain, *"Why are you angry? And why has your countenance fallen? If you do well, will you not be accepted? And if you do not do well, sin lies at the door. And its desire is for you, but you should rule over it." Gen 4: 6, 7 (NKJV)*

Cain is not ready to accept reproof. Instead, he lets anger, resentment, and jealousy ferment within him.

Notice throughout the story Satan isn't mentioned at all. He was there all right, but he was completely out of sight. He doesn't usually announce his presence. He doesn't go out with a bullhorn and say, **"Now hear this! Now hear this! This is Satan speaking."** Satan is far more subtle. He puts his thoughts into our minds that sound so natural that we think the thoughts are our own. We can't keep these thoughts from coming. So far, there is no sin involved. It is only when we began to dwell on these thoughts and let them take root in our hearts that it becomes sin. This is what happened to Cain. Satan whispered in Cain's ear, "Your fruits and vegetables are just as good and valuable as some animal. God should be just as pleased with your vegetables as He is with Abel's animal." Cain listened and let his mind dwell upon the thought. After all, why should God be more pleased with Abel's animals than with my fruits and vegetables? So he makes a decision. He will offer the best of his fruits and vegetables. However, he doesn't consider whether this would be pleasing to God. Now when God is not pleased, Cain again listens to Satan, "God just likes him better than you."

Satan was able to continue to feed Cain enough lies until his hatred finally exploded and he killed his brother Abel. Satan had whispered in Cain's ear, "No one will ever know." However, God saw, He knew and Abel's blood cried to him from the ground.

> And the LORD said unto Cain, Where is Abel your brother? And he replied, I don't know, Am I my brother's keeper?

> And he said, "What have you done?" The voice of your brother's blood cries out to me from the ground. So now you are cursed from the earth, which has opened her mouth to receive your brother's blood from your hand. "When you till the ground, it shall no longer yield its strength to you. A fugitive and a vagabond you shall be on the earth."

> And Cain said unto the LORD, "My punishment is greater than I can bear! Behold, you have driven me out

this day from the face of the earth; I should be hidden from your face; and I shall be a fugitive and a vagabond on the earth; and it shall come to pass, that anyone who finds me will kill me."

And the LORD said unto him, "Therefore anyone who kills Cain, vengeance shall be taken on him sevenfold." And the LORD set a mark upon Cain, lest anyone finding him should kill him.

GEN 4: 9-15

Now when God asked Cain where his brother was, he replied. **"Am I my brother's keeper?"** This has been the classic reply throughout the ages for those who show no compassion or love for others. The spirit of Cain is very much alive and well today. Cain thought that he could get away with murder, but he couldn't. He didn't pay the ultimate price of death because of what he did, but he did pay a terrible price. Satan is still telling people that they can get away with murder. You can be sure that Satan rejoices because of suffering and death in war. He is especially delighted with the murder of the innocents through abortion and the death of Christians through religious wars.

Again, Satan was depressed because God had disappointed him. Satan's plan was flawless and yet, he did not succeed in getting God to destroy Cain. He merely put a mark upon Cain to make sure that no one would kill him. God wanted to make an example of Cain. This was exactly the opposite of what Satan wanted. Again, Satan's plans did not succeed. But what would happen if he could get all mankind to rebel against God, to kill, oppress and destroy each other, to get them to use each other for their own selfish ends? Then surely God would destroy them.

That is what Satan now sought to do. The Bible says that Satan was very successful in this endeavor.

> And GOD saw that the wickedness of man was great in the earth, and that every imagination of the thoughts of his heart was only evil continually.

> And it repented the LORD that he had made man on the earth, and it grieved him at his heart. And the LORD said, I will destroy man whom I have created from the face of the earth; both man, and beast, and the creeping thing, and the birds of the air; for I am sorry that I have made them.
>
> GEN 6: 5-7

That was enough to make Satan jump up and down with glee. But wait, Satan was celebrating too soon. Let's look at the next verse.

> " But Noah found grace in the eyes of the LORD."
>
> GEN 6:8

Satan had overlooked Noah. Noah was a righteous man. He and his family still served the Lord. God would yet be faithful to his promise to Adam and Eve and carry out his plan of redemption through Noah.

> The earth also was corrupt before God, and the earth was filled with violence. And God looked upon the earth, and, behold, it was corrupt; for all flesh had corrupted his way upon the earth.

> And God said unto Noah, "The end of all flesh is come before me; for the earth is filled with violence through them; and, behold, I will destroy them with the earth. Make for yourself an ark of gopher wood;

make rooms in the ark, and cover it with pitch inside and outside.

And this is how you shall build an: The length of the ark shall be three hundred cubits, (about 450 feet) the width of it fifty cubits, (about 75 feet) and the height of it thirty cubits. (About 45 feet) you shall make a window for the ark and in a cubit (about 1.5 ft.) you shall finish it from above; and set the door of the ark in its side; you shall make it with lower, second, and third decks."

And, behold, I, even I, am bringing a flood of waters upon the earth, to destroy all flesh, in which is the breath of life, from under heaven; and every thing that is in the earth shall die, but I will establish my covenant with you; and you shall come into the ark, you, your sons, and your wife, and your sons' wives with thee.

GEN. 6: 11-18

God was going to destroy all mankind in the flood except for Noah and his family. Crestfallen, Satan realizes that if he is going to get God to destroy all mankind, he will have to begin all over again.

CHAPTER 4

BABYLON

Immediately after the flood, Satan lost no time plotting man's destruction. Instead of just trying to get mankind to use and abuse each other for their own selfish ends, he would get them to unite to form a world kingdom with a new religion. He would teach them spiritual things with a new demonic twist. He would teach them about the power of the soul, so that they might perform psychic phenomena and be deceived into believing they were becoming like God.

> And the whole earth used the same language, and the same words. And it came to pass, as they journeyed from the east, that they found a plain in the land of Shinar; and they dwelt there. And they said one to another, come, let us make bricks, and burn them thoroughly. And they had brick for stone, and they used tar for mortar. And they said, come, let us build for ourselves a city and a tower, whose top may reach into heaven; and let us make a name for ourselves, otherwise we be scattered abroad upon the face of the whole earth.

> And the LORD came down to see the city and the tower, which the children of men had built. And the LORD said, "Behold, the people is one, and they have all one language; and this they begin to do: and now

nothing will be restrained from them, which they have imagined to do. Come, let us go down there and confuse their language, that they may not understand one another's speech.

So the LORD scattered them abroad from there upon the face of all the earth: and they stopped building the city. Therefore it's name is called Babel; because there the LORD confused the language of all the earth: and from there the LORD scattered them abroad upon the face of all the earth."

GEN 11: 1-9

Babel or Babylon, as it was later called, became the new center of civilization after the Flood. Since there was only one language and one culture, the people could work together on any project that suited their fancy. They had the advantage of being able to bring into this beginning civilization most of the knowledge and skills of the people before the Flood.

They must have brought with them a keen sense of the weaknesses and failures of the pre-flood civilization. Perhaps one of those weaknesses may have been the fragmentary nature of their society. That could have been one of the main reasons for building a city with a tower to reach up to heaven. They didn't want a fragmented society. They didn't want power bosses and little kingdoms. They wanted one government for all the people, united together to work for the common good of all the people.

It sounds good, doesn't it? It's the perfect formula for a NEW WORLD ORDER. But this is not the kind of world that God wanted for mankind. This world order had man as its center. The people said, "Let us make a name for ourselves." They were trying to make a monument to their glory, not the glory of God. They had given themselves over to idolatry, instead of the worship of the true God. They listened to Satan and began to learn about psychic power. Instead, they should have sought true spiritual power from God. If they were to continue in this pattern, soon all knowledge of the true God would vanish. God could not allow this plan to succeed.

To foil this rebellion, God did not have to destroy the earth again. Instead, he merely confused their language. They could not understand one another so they went off in small groups and formed new tribes and nations

Satan's plan did not work this time, but he liked the plan. He would try it again and again. This plan of Satan would later be called the New World Order. It is the same New World Order of which President Bush and former USSR President Gorbachev spoke.

The Apostle John in the book of Revelation refers to the New World Order religion and calls it Babylon because out of the original Babylon sprang forth a mystery religion, which has been the mother of all mystery religions throughout history

The city of Babylon was founded by Nimrod. Only four generations separated him from the time of the Great Flood. The memories of the pre-flood civilization were still very fresh since those who had survived on the ark were still living. He must have heard many stories about life before the flood, and false religious practices of that day.

This evidently appealed to Nimrod and his lust for power, so he set out to build a tower and make a name for himself. The tower was to be used for worship of false gods. It would also serve to keep the people close so he could rule over them. Little did Nimrod know that he himself would become one of the main sources of the mystery religions of the world.

According to legend, Nimrod had a very beautiful wife by the name of Semiramis. She either killed or had Nimrod killed. She then got pregnant by another man and named the child Tammuz. She claimed that he was actually her dead husband Nimrod who had come back in the form of this child. Thus was born the teaching of reincarnation, which is one of the cornerstones of all Eastern Religions, and seems to be Satan's favorite doctrine.

The image of this mother and son has appeared on statues and murals all over the ancient world and even today. The Madonna was not originally a Christian symbol, but an idolatrous one. This mother and son were known in Egypt as Isis and Osiris; in India, she is known as Isi or Parvati and her son as Ishwara. She was Ashtoreth, or Astarte, to the Canaanites; Diana to the Ephesians; and Venus to the Romans.

These were not the only gods of the Babylonians. They had many gods. They had gods of wind and rain, sun, moon, stars, heat, cold, water, fire, trees and animals.

One of the most important religions was Pantheism. Pantheism is the belief that god is everything and everything is god. That means that man is a part of god. That is where New Agers of today get some of their ideas. They believe that they will keep being born again, and again, and again, until they get it right and become a part of the universal god; the FORCE of the universe. It was no accident that the "Star Wars" movie series prominently displayed a new religion called the FORCE.

These religious ideas of ancient Babylon are also expressed in what is today referred to as Humanism. The people said, "Let us build ourselves a city and a tower . . . let us make a name for ourselves". The city was for their pride, the tower for their new religions and the name for themselves. Humanism is basically an attempt to make man the center of all things and ultimately to push God off his throne and take over. This is the old lie of Satan in the Garden of Eden, "and ye shall be as gods". It's an old lie but every generation hears it again.

Humanism, with its amoral philosophy, has invaded every strata of society in America today. It has destroyed our public schools. It has corrupted and perverted our legal system. It has rendered the general public completely confused as to what is right and wrong, or whether there is such a thing as right and wrong.

ENVIRONMENTALISM is a natural extension of Pantheism. If God is everything and everything is God; then people, animals, trees, grass, water, and fish, are all a part of God. For environmentalists, one of the greatest of sins you can commit is to do anything harmful to Mother Nature, because you have attacked their god. By attacking their god, you have attacked them.

The religion of Pantheism traveled from Babylon to many other countries, most notably India. There some people would not hesitate to kill you if they saw you kill a rat that was stealing your child's food. They are very careful not to kill any animal. They would not even swat a fly. Many of them are even careful where they walk; they might step on an ant.

In the United States these people worship Mother Nature. They think nothing about aborting human babies or even killing the old people, but they must do everything possible to save the whales, baby seals, snail darters and even butterflies. They consider human beings a virus on Mother Earth. Their numbers must be reduced and their environmental impact muted and controlled.

FEMINISM is also a Babylonian concept. They not only had male gods, but also female goddesses of sex and fertility. They worshiped these sex goddesses by having temple virgins with whom the worshipers had sex orgies. The same is true today. Feminism is not primarily about equal rights as many are led to believe, but about the freedom of female independence. They want to be able to have sex without the responsibility of babies. They also want to have a life and career independent of a man. This feminist spirit despises marriage, family, and children. It also supports sexual awareness, a perverted sexual education, and abortion.

From his viewpoint, Satan had a good thing going in Babel and he knew it. Unfortunately from Satan's point of view God didn't destroy man, but only confused his language and scattered him abroad. "Next time," no doubt Satan said to the demon hordes, "next time". However, Satan was not about to give up. He and his demon hordes would continue to work on the people scattered abroad, until God would get so disgusted with them that He would have to destroy them. Satan was soon to find out though that God took his promise to Adam and Eve seriously.

CHAPTER 5

THE STRUGGLE CONTINUES

After Babel, it almost seemed as though Satan might have won after all. The language of the people was confused. They were scattered over the face of the earth, but they still clung to their worship of false gods. Generations came and went. Finally, God found the man he was looking for. In the city of Ur, God chose a man to carry out his plan. This man would become the ancestor of the promised Savior (the woman's seed).

> Now the LORD had said unto Abram, go forth out of your country, and from your relatives, and from thy father's house, into a land that I will show thee: And I will make of you a great nation, and I will bless you, and make your name great; and you shall be a blessing: And I will bless them that bless you, and curse him that curses you: and in you shall all families of the earth be blessed.
>
> GEN 12: 1-3

Why God chose Abram (who was later called Abraham) to carry out his plan. We really don't know. However, we do know the type of man God needed to accomplish his purpose. He needed a man who sought after the truth. Most people don't seek after the truth. They simply accept whatever their friends, family, and teachers tell them. I believe that anyone who truly seeks the truth will find it.

When God revealed Himself to Abraham, Abraham listened. Very often it is hard to get people to listen to the truth. Their minds are so filled with all the garbage they have heard they don't have any room for the truth. Abraham was a man who was not only willing to listen, but also discarded all the garbage.

The Bible says this about him, *"Abraham believed God, and it was counted unto him for righteousness." Romans 4:3* God put Abraham through very severe tests. God promised to make Abraham a great nation, but Abraham had to wait 30 years for the promised son to be born. You can be sure that Satan had a hand in Sarah's impatience when she told Abraham to take Hagar and have a child by her. Since Hagar was Sarah's servant, any child she had would belong to Sarah. This mistake produced Ishmael, the father of the Arabs. They have been a thorn in the side of Israel ever since, but through it all, Abraham remained faithful.

Satan now turns his attention to Abraham's descendants. Jacob's son Joseph interpreted the dream of Pharaoh, King of Egypt, revealing that there was going to be seven years of plenty followed by seven years of famine. Pharaoh puts Joseph in charge of storing away food during the seven good years so there will be food during the seven years of famine. When the famine came, Jacob and the rest of his family go to Egypt. Pharaoh provided for them the land of Goshen (a part of Egypt) where they could tend to their cattle and sheep.

They find great favor in Egypt to begin with because of Joseph. After a number of generations later the Egyptians forgot about Joseph and the rulers of Egypt become concerned.

The Israelites were having too many kids. Some day they might join with Egypt's enemies. The Egyptians then decided to make the Israelites slaves and they attempted to destroy all the boy babies that were born.

Satan must have been quite pleased by this turn of events, but then God raised up Moses to lead the children of Israel out of Egypt and bring them to the land God had promised to Abraham.

Pharaoh was not about to let the children of Israel go easily. However, after a series of plagues that God sends upon Egypt, he finally agreed to let them go. Then he changed his mind and sent his army after them. The children of Israel were trapped between the army of Egypt and the Red Sea. God set a cloud and pillar of fire between the Israelites and Egyptians. God had Moses stretch out his rod over the water. The water parted and the children of Israel were able to pass through the sea on dry ground. After the Israelites were safely on the other side, God removed the cloud. When the Egyptians tried to pass over, their chariot wheels got stuck. God had Moses stretch out the rod over the water again. The water came back together and the Egyptians were drowned. Once more Satan's plans were foiled, but he didn't give up. There would be plenty more opportunities to destroy them.

During the forty years the children of Israel spent in the desert on the way to the Promised Land, Satan was quite busy stirring up fear, doubt, idolatry, and rebellion. If I had been in charge I probably would have destroyed them, but God didn't. Who can understand the depths of His love or the wonders of His patience and mercy? Satan failed again.

Over the centuries Israel would provoke God again and again. God would send famines and let their enemies oppress them, but He would not allow anyone to completely destroy them. God is faithful. God made a promise to Adam and Eve. He made a promise to Noah. He made a promise to Abraham, Isaac, Jacob, Judah, and David. He promised that a child born of a woman would crush the head of the serpent. That promise would be fulfilled.

The Bible says,

> "But when the fullness of the time was come, God sent forth his Son, made of a woman, made under the law, to redeem them that were under the law, that we might receive the adoption of sons.
>
> GAL 4:4, 5

Satan did not understand God's plan of salvation for mankind, but he did know that salvation was to come through this child which was to be born in Bethlehem. Satan knew that it had been prophesied that he would be defeated by this child. He certainly wasn't going to let that happen if he could help it.

After Jesus was born, Wise Men from the East come to Israel in order that they might pay homage and worship the newborn King. They expected to find him in Jerusalem the capital city. When they began to inquire where the newborn King might be, they were brought to see King Herod. Herod quickly calls for his advisors who tell him that it had been prophesied the Messiah would be born in Bethlehem.

This now was Satan's chance to destroy the promised seed. He quickly planted the thought in Herod's mind to kill this child of promise. So Herod called the Wise Men and told them to go and search for the child. He asked them to report back to him when they found him he might also go and worship him. After the Wise Men had given their gifts to Jesus and worshiped Him they started back home. God warned them in a dream not to report back to Herod. They then returned home by a different route. When Herod realized what had happened he decided to kill all the children in Bethlehem two years old and younger.

In the meantime, God instructed Joseph to take Mary and Jesus and go to Egypt. They stayed in Egypt until after Herod died. When they returned to Israel they decided to live in Nazareth where they felt safer. That was the first time Satan would try to destroy Jesus, but it wouldn't be the last time.

After Jesus began his ministry Satan again tried to kill Him by causing a great storm while they were in a boat on the Sea of Galilee. At another time Satan incited the multitude to try to throw Jesus off a cliff.

Finally, Satan got his chance. Jesus and His disciples came to Jerusalem to worship at the time of the Passover. Satan convinced Judas, one of Jesus' disciples to betray Him. He motivated the High Priest to condemn Jesus and used the cowardice of Pilate to crucify Him. Oh, how Satan, the evil angels, and the demonic hordes of hell must have rejoiced to see Jesus on that cross. Then right before He died He said, *"It is finished."* I believe that when Jesus spoke those words stark fear suddenly engulfed Satan. Satan now knew that he had made a mistake. When Jesus said it is finished he was proclaiming that the work that the Father sent Him to do had been completed. He had borne the sin of all mankind making it possible for them to return to the Father's love.

The death of Jesus on the cross was not the end of the story, it was just the beginning. Early Sunday morning Jesus rose from the dead and paid a visit to hell where he declared victory. What the hordes of hell thought was victory was in fact their defeat.

The Bible says,

> "But we speak the wisdom of God in a mystery, even the hidden wisdom, which God ordained before the world unto our glory: Which none of the princes of this world knew: for had they known it, they would not have crucified the Lord of glory." 1

COR. 2: 7, 8

Satan had been outmaneuvered. This time he had failed worse than ever. The very thing that God had promised to Adam and Eve had just been fulfilled. How could he have been so blind not to see what was happening? Would he give up? Never! Now was the time for damage control. Maybe he could still win. If not he would do his best to get as many humans on his side as possible. In the meantime he would redouble his efforts to destroy every human being he possibly could.

CHAPTER 6

DAMAGE CONTROL
(Satan's Attempt to regain his power)

The First 500 Years:

The word quickly spread that Jesus had risen from the dead and that He had appeared to over 500 people at one time. When Pentecost came and the Holy Spirit was poured out upon Jesus disciples Peter then preached to the multitudes. Three thousand people believed on Jesus that very day. In the days that followed more and more people were added to this group. Satan had no trouble convincing the Jewish leaders that this movement must be stopped. Persecution against the Church broke out in Jerusalem and the believers fled. The problem is that wherever they went, they took the message of Jesus with them. The message they proclaimed spread like wildfire. All Satan had been able to accomplish was to scatter the fire.

The Jewish leaders continued to persecute the Jewish Christians, but now the Gentiles were also becoming believers. Soon Satan had Roman leaders convinced that these Christians were a dangerous religious sect which needed to be put down.

The Romans didn't understand Christians because they did not worship idols but a god that could not be seen therefore the Romans considered Christians to be atheists. Because

Christians would not worship Caesar they considered them guilty of treason. Christians also celebrated the Lords Supper therefore the Romans considered them to be cannibals.

It wasn't long before Satan had the Romans slaughtering the Christians in sports arenas before huge crowds because they would not deny Christ. Some Christians were hung on crosses, covered with naphtha and set on fire. Some were placed in arenas covered with animal skins to be torn in pieces by wild beasts. Yet no matter how horribly these Christians suffered, they would not give up their faith. Not only that, the more the Christians were persecuted, the more they seemed to multiply. Some people were saying that the blood of the martyrs was the seed of the Church.

So far Satan was having only limited success in trying to destroy the Church. Then in 312 AD the Emperor Constantine claimed to have had a vision in which he saw a cross in the sky and he heard a voice which said, "With this sign conquer." Following, this vision, he ordered a Christian Cross to be painted on his soldiers' shields. Under this emblem, Constantine was successful in battle and entered Rome.

We don't know whether Constantine actually had this vision or not, but he did decided to quit persecuting the church and to rule over it instead.

It has been said, "If you can't lick them, join them." Satan decided that if he couldn't destroy Christianity outright, he would subvert it. It wasn't very long until Theodosius became emperor and Satan inspired him to make Christianity the state religion. In 392 AD, he declared all heathen sacrifices to be high treason.

After this the pagans were made Christians by force. The Roman soldiers rounded people up like cattle and herded them to the river to be baptized. Unfortunately, while the pagans were being converted and becoming Christians, paganism was also coming into the churches. If Satan could not stop the proclamation of the Gospel, he would do all in his power to pollute the Gospel so as to make it ineffective.

Many of the newly converted clung to their heathen ways and practices. The churches were already giving special honor to those who had been martyred and were proclaiming them to be saints. After this, it was a simple matter to substitute idols and false gods for saints and relics. The veneration of Mary came a little later but was soon accompanied with the statues and pictures of Madonna. We have already explained the heathen origin of the Madonna. This Madonna now came to be venerated as Mary and Jesus. The corruption that had gradually been coming into the Church now multiplied.

Soon the celebration of the resurrection of Jesus was renamed Easter in honor of Ashtoreth, the fertility Canaanite goddess. Peter rabbit, Easter eggs, and the Easter bunny were all from idol worship. They all had to do with heathen fertility religions. The fact that these traditions continue even in the churches of today is incredible.

The celebration of the birth of Jesus was likewise trashed. First of all, Jesus was not born on the 25th of December. Of this we can be certain. This day was selected because the newly converted worshiped one of their idols at this time of year. It was the time of the winter solstice. An evergreen tree was also used in this worship - hence the Christmas tree. Santa Clause was a later figment of the imagination. Saint Nicholas was brought into the celebration because he was considered a patron saint of children.

By this time Satan and all the devils in hell must have been jumping up and down for joy. Finally he seemed to be getting somewhere with these Christians. If he could not outright destroy them, at least he was able to corrupt them. Then Satan pulled out his bigger guns and aimed at the church leaders. He would use their envy, greed, and lust for power to keep the Church from carrying out the mission which Christ assigned to it.

As we mentioned earlier, the church had already been compromised by the forced conversions of pagans and had also begun to hold saints and relics as sacred. However, a far bigger problem was soon to become evident and that was the struggle for power.

The Church had been born in the Roman Empire. The Roman Empire ruled from the top down. Now the Bishop of Rome wanted this same kind of power. However, the bishops in various other cities also wanted that power for themselves.

In 385 AD Siricius became Bishop of Rome and claimed universal jurisdiction over the Church. He was not able to achieve his goals because in 395 AD the Roman Empire was divided, with the Western capital at Rome and the Eastern capital at Constantinople. This made it very difficult for the Roman Bishop to get the Eastern part of the Empire to recognize his authority. Later Roman bishops also tried to gain this recognition, but the Ecumenical Council of Chalcedon in 451 AD gave the Patriarch of Constantinople equal status with the Bishop of Rome

After the Western part of the Roman Empire fell before the barbarian hordes of the North in 476 AD, the churches became islands of stability in a sea of turmoil. The Church began to convert the invaders and soon the formerly barbarian hordes were in submission to the Pope. The Popes took advantage of the situation to form alliances to their advantage and gradually the Popes became the greatest authority in the West.

As the first five centuries of the Christian Church came to an end, Satan must have felt discouraged. Yes, he had won some battles, but he had not won the war. He had his fun as Christians were being torn to pieces by wild beasts. He had taken great delight as Christians became human torches. But he had not been able to destroy the Christian Church. In fact the more Christians he killed, the faster the church grew. When Satan realized that he could not destroy the Church through persecution, he decided to weaken and corrupt the church. He was able to accomplish this by getting the emperor of Rome to declare Christianity the official state religion. By forcing the pagans to become Christians, he brought paganism into the Church. Satan then used ambition and greed of church officials to further corrupt the church. And yet for all of this, the church continued to grow, the Gospel was preached, and many were still faithful to Jesus. The Gospel of Jesus Christ had now been preached in Africa, Asia, India, Europe, and the British Isles. Satan had not yet accomplished his purposes. He would have to redouble his efforts.

THE SECOND 500 YEARS TO 1000 AD

Satan's plan to destroy the Church and mankind for the next 500 years centered mainly in two areas. First, Satan would continue to use blind ambition of church leaders to centralize power. He would use their oversized egos to force their ideas on the rest of the Church. As long as pastors were able to read the Word of God and allow the Holy Spirit to bring the interpretation, Satan's work was hindered. In order to fully corrupt the Church it was necessary for the authority to interpret Scripture be in the hands of the hierarchy only.

The second part of Satan's plan for the next 500 years was to have a rival religious system which would compete with Christianity. Paganism would not work. Christianity had already overcome paganism although remnants of paganism had been incorporated into the Church. It was in fact the paganism still remaining in the church that allowed Satan to set up a new religion. This new religion would come against paganism much more strongly than Christianity ever had. Before we look at this new religion, we will first observe Satan's attack upon the Church from within.

As we observed during the last five hundred years, Satan was using the blind ambition, greed and lust for power to bring about a centralization of the Church. It was necessary for Satan to have a concentration of power in the Church so that he could control it. At the end of the fifth century, both the Bishops of Rome and of Constantinople were competing for power. But in 533 AD, Justinian who was at that time emperor of the eastern branch of the Roman Empire issued his famous decree making the Bishop of Rome the head of all Christendom. This date, 533 AD, might well be considered the real beginning of the Papacy.

It has been well said, "Power corrupts and absolute power corrupts absolutely." This is exactly what followed in the church world.

In order to establish full control and authority the Papacy was led by Satan not only to assume authority in the Church, but also in the civil realm. In the year A.D. 800, as

Charles the Great, also called Charlemagne, was attending a Christmas service Pope Leo placed a crown upon his head and proclaimed him Emperor of the Romans. Immediately the assembled people shouted their acclamation. It is reported that Charles was not too happy about this, but he did accept the title and had his subjects take a new oath of allegiance to him as emperor. In this way, the Pope took upon himself the authority to appoint kings and emperors. In the following centuries, the Papacy gained more and more power in the civil realm. If kings did not do what he wanted them to, he would excommunicate them and command the priests not to perform any baptisms, marriages, or funerals in that country. Soon the whole country was coming against the ruler, and he would have to concede to the will of the Pope.

The power and authority that the Popes exercised in the civil arena would hardly compare with the totalitarian control they had over the Church. The Pope demanded that all churches and pastors acknowledge his supremacy. Any churches or pastors that refused he declared to be on the road to hell, and advocated the death penalty for heresy. In the following paragraphs some of the things that the Popes did to consolidate their power are described in the following paragraphs.

SUPPRESSION OF THE BIBLE:
In the first few centuries of the Christian Church the Bible could easily be read by the common people, because the New Testament was written in Greek and the Old Testament had been translated from the Hebrew into Greek. Any educated person in the Roman Empire knew and used Greek in business and commerce. After a few centuries, things changed. By

the fourth century many people in the Western part of the Roman Empire had forgotten Greek and were instead using Latin in business transactions. In order to meet this changing need for the Bible to be available for the people to read, it was translated into Latin. This translation, which eventually became the standard Bible of the Western Church, was called the Vulgate. Vulgate is a Latin word that means common or popular. The Vulgate is largely attributed to Saint Jerome, who completed his part of the translation in 405 AD.

While the Vulgate means common, it soon became common only for the Roman priesthood. After the Gothic tribes of the north invaded the Empire, the Latin language quickly became a dead language and the only people who could read it was the priesthood and others who were University educated. Even this was not enough to satisfy the Papacy. To make sure that only the priesthood would be able to dispense the Word of God, the Bibles were chained to the pulpit and no one but a priest was allowed to read it. All translations of the Bible into the common languages of the people were forbidden.

PERVERSION OF THE SCRIPTURE:

They didn't try to change the words of the Bible, but they perverted it by inventing doctrines to be taught along side of and instead of the pure teaching of the Word of God. The Roman Church teaches that there are other sources of revelation and doctrine which even supersedes the Bible. Besides the Bible, they draw their doctrine and teachings from traditions, councils and the pronouncement of the Pope when he speaks in his official capacity as the Vicar of Christ.

Some of the inventions of the Papacy are: Purgatory, the Veneration of the Saints, Indulgences, Mariolatry, Worship of the Host, Salvation through Works, Penance, Celibacy, the Priesthood, and various superstitions. The most glaring teaching is the primacy of the Bishop of Rome.

PREEMINENCE OF ROME BASED ON PETER:

No doubt the Bishop of Rome was first considered to be above the other Bishops because Rome was the seat of the Roman Empire. When the seat of the Roman Empire moved to Constantinople in AD 330, the Bishops of Rome wanted to keep their preeminence. It was at this time they declared that the Apostle Peter was the first Bishop of Rome; giving Rome the preeminence. The Bible does not state that Peter was ever in Rome, nor is there a tradition that claims that Peter even preached in Rome. There is a tradition that says Peter was arrested and taken to Rome where he was crucified upside down, because he did not feel worthy to die the same way Jesus did.

Nevertheless, the Church at Rome based their preeminence on Peter. They proclaimed that Peter was given the Keys of the Kingdom; that he was the first Bishop of Rome; and that he passed down the authority of the Keys of the Kingdom to the next Bishop of Rome from whom the whole Church receives its authority to preach the Gospel. This formed the basis for the teaching of Apostolic Succession.

It is true that Jesus did give the Keys of the Kingdom to Peter in Matthew 16: 19, *"And I will give unto thee the keys of the kingdom of heaven: and whatever you shall bind on earth shall be bound in heaven: and whatever you shall loose on earth shall be loosed in heaven."*

This authority however, was not just given to Peter. It was also given to the other Apostles and to the whole Church as we see in the following Scriptures, which were spoken to all the disciples:

Matthew 18:18 Verily I say unto you, whatever you shall bind on earth shall be bound in heaven: and whatever you shall loose on earth shall be loosed in heaven.

> John 20: 21 Then said Jesus to them again, Peace be unto you: as my Father hath sent me, even so I send you. 22 When he had said this, he breathed on them, and said to them, Receive the Holy Spirit: 23 Those to whom you forgive sins, they are forgiven; and those who do not receive your forgiveness, they are not forgiven.

While the Western Church in Rome made their claims based on Peter, the Eastern Church with its leadership in Constantinople rejected these claims. Tensions continued to grow between the Eastern and Western Church until the year 1054 when the Pope at Rome excommunicated the patriarch of Constantinople and the patriarch summoned a council and excommunicated the Pope.

THE POPES CLAIMED FOR THEMSELVES THE SUPREME AUTHORITY TO SPEAK FOR CHRIST:

The Roman Church continued to make their claim to power and authority based on Peter. On the basis of this assumed authority, they declared that if anyone claimed God as Father he also had to acknowledge the Church as his mother, (by mother they meant the Church of Rome). By the sixth century Gregory I claimed that he was the chief of all Bishops, that he was the bishop of the whole Church, divinely appointed to be Christ's only representative on earth. After this, the Bishops of Rome assumed the name Pope as their title, which means papa or father.

The Pope was declared to be the Vicar of Christ and as such spoke for Christ. If anyone would not acknowledge the authority of the Papacy, he was considered a renegade and outside of the Kingdom of God. If anyone dared to preach the Gospel who did not have the blessings of the Roman Church, he was considered a heretic, even if what he preached was true. Not only that, but anyone who possessed even a small portion of the Bible could be put to death.

THEY USED EVERY MEANS POSSIBLE TO BRING THE WHOLE CHURCH UNDER THEIR CONTROL:

While outright persecution and the killing of heretics was fairly rare during the years preceding A.D. 1000, the Popes used every other means of persuasion and intimidation to bring all churches and ministers under his authority. The most notable example of this occurred in Great Britain.

England and Scotland were Christianized by Roman soldiers in the first couple of centuries. The Celtic race accepted Christianity with great enthusiasm. They established monasteries and did missionary work in Europe. Celtic Christianity spread rapidly in Europe and it appeared for a time as though it might become the dominant form in Europe. Later, St. Patrick ministered in Ireland from A.D. 431 to A.D. 461, where he brought many more people to Christ.

The Roman Church, however, was not well pleased. Pope Gregory the Great wanted all the Christians in Great Britain to be under his authority, therefore he sent Benedictine monks to carry on missionary propaganda. He finally obtained his goal and in 596 AD, he sent Augustine and forty other

Benedictine monks to England to the Court of King Ethelbert of Kent. In 597 AD, Augustine baptized King Ethelbert and thereby won all his subjects. The rest of England, Scotland, and Ireland still followed the Iro-Celtic form of Christianity. Finally Rome sent Wilfrid, a British Benedictine Monk, who turned the tide in favor of Rome. At the Synod of Whitby in 664 AD, the differences were settled in favor of Rome.

SATAN'S OTHER PLAN:

While Satan was no doubt pleased about the progress he had been making in the Christian Church, he wanted more. Satan was not satisfied to just dominate, corrupt and pervert the Church; he wanted to completely destroy it. For this reason, he decided to set up a rival religion in competition with the church. Satan was greatly aided in this by the Church itself.

Since Christians had embraced the adoration of Mary and the Saints, it could easily be construed that they were worshiping idols. The Jews worshiped one God. The Christians also worshiped one God. A Christian though understood God to be one God but three persons; Father, Son, and Holy Spirit. No doubt this was confusing to people who had been involved in idol worship. Satan would make use of this in devising a new religion.

ISLAM:

In a country now called Saudi Arabia, a man named Mohammed was born of the house of Koreish. He was in line for governorship of Mecca. However, when his grandfather died, the governorship passed to another branch of the family.

Mohammed was a merchant trader and camel driver who often encountered Christians and Jews. He had picked up many of their ideas. He evidently was fascinated with the Old Testament Scriptures. He realized that he was descended from Abraham and considered Jesus a great prophet, but he totally rejected the worship of Mary, the Saints and relics. In the city of Mecca where he grew up and lived, there were temples with many idols. The most prominent among them was the moon god who was called Allah. That is the reason one of the symbols of Islam is the crescent moon.

Soon Mohammed had developed his own religion called Islam. It is a curious mixture of Jewish, Christian and Pagan religions. When he was about forty, he began teaching his new religion. He claimed that the angel Gabriel appeared to him in a vision and revealed all these things to him. At first, he just confided in friends and relatives. After four years, he had about forty followers. Then he began to receive ridicule and persecution in his hometown of Mecca, so he fled to Medina in 622 AD. This is the year the followers of Islam use to begin their calendar.

No doubt Mohammed felt anger and humiliation for having to flee from Mecca. Satan was able to use this to mold the religion of Islam into one of the most intolerant and bloodthirsty religions in history. Islam is a religion of hate, spread by the sword. It has encouraged slavery, polygamy, and the degradation of women.

In Medina, Mohammed gained many followers and assembled an army that he first used to conquer Mecca in 630 AD. Mohammed is said to have destroyed three hundred and sixty idols there. Even though Mohammed died in A.D. 632, his religion didn't. The Islamic army went on to conquer Syria in 634; Jerusalem in 637; Egypt in 638; Persia in 640; North Africa in 689; and Spain in 711 AD.

From Spain, they pushed on into France. Islam's aim was to overrun all of Europe from West to East. They came very close to conquering Europe, and they might have succeeded except for Charles Martel, the grandfather of Charlemagne. In 732 AD, Islam was driven back with a loss of about 350,000. Charles the Great completed the work of Charles Martel in driving Islam back. The armies of Islam though had already treaded upon thousands of Christian churches in Africa, and Asia. Now much of Europe also lay in ruins.

After about 150 years the Islamic Arabs stopped their conquests for a time; but Islam would continue through the centuries to dominate, enslave, and persecute all who would not submit to Allah.

SATAN'S SCORECARD:

How has Satan scored at the end of the first millennium? Yes, there were many things Satan was no doubt happy about. Satan had succeeded in getting men of the Church to lust after and compete for power. He had succeeded in getting all the main churches under the authority of Rome. He had brought idolatry and pagan practices into the Church. He had succeeded in making the Bible rare for the individual Christian, and he had perverted its teachings. He had also succeeded in bringing forth a rival religion to replace Christianity. Islam had, for the most part, replaced Christianity in Africa, Egypt, the whole Middle East, Asia Minor, and what is now Turkey.

Yet, the Christian Church remained in Russia, Greece, and Western Europe. Satan had not yet accomplished his goal of destroying Christianity and bringing all mankind under his control. One thing he could take great satisfaction in was that all the Western Church was now under Rome. Satan would take great advantage of that fact in the centuries to follow.

THE THIRD 500 YEARS, FROM 1000 TO 1500 AD:

At the beginning of the new millennium, it was time for Satan to take stock of where he was and to make plans for the future. He had won some battles, but he had not won the war. Satan's hatred for God burned within him. He detested the creatures God placed on this earth. He hated the fact that God's plan for mankind was still intact; and that if God's plan succeeded, mankind could still grab the glory and honor that Satan felt he deserved.

After all Satan, who had once been called Lucifer or light bearer, considered himself the most beautiful and powerful of all the angels. Now why would God want to make a man? No, this must not stand! Satan felt that he deserved the praise, honor and worship. Since God made man, Satan felt he must get man on his side so that man would worshiped him instead of God. If he could not get mankind to worship him, then he would have to keep men from worshiping God. What he really wanted to do was to kill all mankind, but God would not allow that. So what was he now to do?

First of all, he would try to keep the world in turmoil. He just loved it when they came against each other and the blood flowed. He loved it when the Muslims went forth to conquer the world for Allah. Unfortunately, the Arabs had lost their zeal. They wanted to settle down and enjoy their peace and prosperity. This wouldn't do. Satan decided to stir up the Turks and get them to take up the fight. This is just what he did.

In 1057 AD, four Turkish Sultans began a new conquest of the world for Allah. They invaded the Middle East and conquered all the Arab lands, Palestine, and Syria. The Turks crushed the armies of the Eastern Roman Empire, which was now called the Byzantine Empire. In 1095 AD, the Byzantine Emperor Alexius Comnenus asked Urban II, the Pope of Rome, to help him fight the Turks. Pope Urban II decided to help and called for a holy crusade against the infidels.

In 1096 AD, the First Crusade began. At Constantinople the Crusaders joined the Byzantine forces and in 1097 AD, the combined army defeated the Muslims at Nicaea, in what is now northwest Turkey. Crusaders then separated and marched to Jerusalem where they arrived in the summer of 1099 AD. After six weeks of fighting they recovered the Holy City. Most of the Crusaders then returned home but the leaders stayed and divided the conquered land into four states. In 1144 AD the Turks conquered one of these states, which in turn led to the Second Crusade. In 1187 AD, Saladin, the Sultan of Egypt and Syria, defeated the Christian army and took back Jerusalem. These crusades finally ended in 1254 AD.

Without a doubt, Satan must have been very happy about all the blood that had been shed in the crusades, but he was not satisfied. He wanted more bloodshed. It was time to consolidate and take advantage of what he had accomplished in previous centuries. The Popes had always been jealous of their authority. It wasn't very difficult for Satan to persuade the Popes to stamp out all false religions and Christian groups which were not subject to the authority of Rome.

The Waldenses were among the first to be persecuted. The Waldenses were members of a Christian group founded by Peter Waldo, a wealthy merchant of Lyon, France. In 1173

AD, he gave his fortune to the church and charity and began to preach on the streets of Lyon. His message of poverty and religious devotion attracted many followers. At first Pope Alexander III approved of the Waldenses preachers (called Paupers) but his successor Pope Lucius III forbid them to preach. In 1184 he excommunicated them and banished them from Lyon. In 1197 full scale persecution broke out. In spite of all the persecution, there still exists about 50,000 Waldenses today. They are found in parts of Europe, Argentina, Uruguay, and in the United States at Valdese, North Carolina.

Satan found the perfect vehicle to carry out this persecution though with Pope Innocent III. He came to power in 1198 A.D. and has been considered to be the most powerful Pope in Church history. He claimed to be the "Vicar of Christ", Supreme Sovereign over the Church and the world, and claimed the right to depose kings and princes. The Kings of Germany, France, England and practically all the other Monarchs of Europe obeyed him. It has been said that no one in history has exercised more power. He ordered the extermination of heretics and began the Inquisition.

In 1208 Innocent III began a crusade against the Waldenses and the Albigenses. The Albigenses was a sectarian group in southern France and parts of Germany and Italy. They believed that all worldly things including their own bodies were evil. Only the spirit was good. They preached against the immorality of the priesthood, pilgrimages, the worship of saints and images, and rejected the claims of the clergy and the Church of Rome. They read the Bible and led morally pure, self-denying lives. While most Christians would not agree with many of their beliefs, it was hardly a reason to order their massacre. A bloody war of extermination was ordered against them. Town after town was put to the sword, and the people were murdered without distinction of age or sex. In spite of all the persecution, the Albigenses were still in existence until after 1350 AD.

The Inquisition was started by Innocent III and perfected in 1231 by Pope Gregory IX. The Inquisition was a Church Court for the detection and punishment of heretics. Everyone was required to inform against heretics. Anyone suspected of being a heretic was subjected to torture in order to extract a confession, without even knowing who his accuser was. Once the victim was sufficiently tortured until a confession was extracted he was turned over to civil authorities for life imprisonment or to be burned at the stake. The victim's property was seized and divided between the Church and the State. The Inquisition was later used against the Protestants and continued with the Spanish Inquisition until 1834 AD, when it was finally suppressed.

The Inquisition was in full swing, and it looked like the Pope was about to gain complete control over the Church; when trouble arose in England. John Wyclif, a Doctor of Theology in Oxford was coming against the doctrine of transubstantiation. Gregory XI ordered the Archbishop and the Bishop of London to make an investigation.

Wyclif was summoned before an ecclesiastical court in the chapel of the Archbishop's palace in 1378; but fearing public sentiment, the trial came to nothing. The English Parliament protected him. Wyclif was respected by both the King and the people of England. He was no longer able to lecture publicly on the subject, so he picked up his pen and began to write. He finally resigned his professorship at Oxford, but continued to carry on a vigorous campaign by means of tracts and sermons. One of his great accomplishments was the translation of the Bible into the English language, which was completed in 1380. His opponents tried to destroy the Bibles, but there are still about 150 manuscripts in existence. Wyclif died December 31, 1384. His followers continued to preach the gospel, but in 1401, heresy was made a capital crime in England. The mere possession of his writings was punishable by death. His teachings were now suppressed by force.

The Council of Constance declared him to be a heretic, his books were burned, and in 1427 they even dug up his body and burned it. They were finally able to burn his body but they could not destroy his influence and his work and teachings continued to be promoted by John Huss of Bohemia.

John Hus was a professor at University of Prague. He became a follower of Wyclif and was head of the reform movement in Bohemia. He was also a powerful preacher and occupied the most influential pulpit in Prague. After 1409 he became the head of the National Bohemian Party in the University. The whole nation rallied around him and the cause of church reform. He was excommunicated and summoned before the Council of Constance, where he was condemned as a heretic and burned at the stake in 1415. This caused an uproar and rebellion throughout all of Bohemia. This rebellion led to what were called the Hussite wars in which the followers of Huss not only repelled the armies of the Crusaders but carried the war into the neighboring countries. The war finally ended in 1433 when concessions were made to the Bohemians at the Council of Basal; when the Hussite danger had passed, Pope Pius II in 1462 declared the papal part of the compact not binding.

As we approach the end of the 15th century, there are
several things we should note. In 1453, Constantinople (the
capital of the Eastern Roman Empire and the head of the
Eastern Orthodox Church) fell to the Islamic Turks and was
renamed Istanbul. The Eastern Orthodox Church was reduced
mainly to the churches in Russia, Greece, and Eastern Europe
although there were also a few churches scattered among
Islamic lands.

The Renaissance (a revival of education, learning,
art, literature, and national pride) began in Italy in 1333
and gradually spread over Europe. The Renaissance was
inspired partly by coming into contact with Middle
Easterners through the Crusades and partly through trade
with the Far East. It was this desire for trade with China
that led Christopher Columbus to embark upon a voyage
which led to the discovery of the New World in 1492. The
Renaissance was also speeded up when the Islamic Turks
took Constantinople. Constantinople had been the center
of Greek culture and learning. When the Turks came in, the
University professors fled to the West.

Before we close out the 15th century, there's one more
thing of which we should take note. There was a man in
Florence, Italy by the name of Savonarola. He was a powerful
preacher against the love of pleasure and sinful practices
among the people and clergy. The Pope at first tried to bribe
him by offering to make him a cardinal, but Savonarola replied
that he wanted no Red Hat except that of a martyr stained
with his own blood. He did not have long to wait. He was
condemned as a heretic and sentenced to death by burning.
That was on May 23, 1498. He died calmly and quietly with
a prayer upon his lips; but before his death, he prophesied:

"The reformation of the church will come soon; already the light begins to dawn."

The years 1000 to 1500 AD have been referred to in history as the dark ages. They might also be referred to as the centuries of blood. Much blood was spilled through the Crusades and more blood was shed through the Inquisition. How many countless thousands of lives were destroyed no one knows, but it was considerable. The shedding of blood no doubt pleased Satan. He could also take great satisfaction in his many other accomplishments during the centuries. He had motivated Gregory VII to strictly enforce the Celibacy of the Clergy. This alone was guaranteed to cause a great deal of immorality in the church. Then Satan inspired the invention of purgatory. It was said to be a place of suffering where one had to pay for all the sins they had committed after being baptized. According to their teaching, the Pope held the keys to the Kingdom and could forgive anyone he wanted to. The Pope had now found an easy way to raise money. All he had to do was to sell indulgences (pieces of paper which proclaimed the forgiveness of sins).

Satan could now congratulate himself. Through these teachings the church members were kept in fear of punishment. They didn't know and understand God's love or forgiveness through the shed blood of Christ Jesus. They lived in constant fear and dread; which, by its very nature, kept them from praising and worshiping God. This was very satisfying to Satan, but every time he thought he had everything under control, someone else would start reading the Bible. This had to be stopped. All religious authority had to be centered in the Pope so that Satan could control it. At the end of the 15th century, it looked like Satan had finally succeeded. The

Albigenses had been exterminated. The Waldenses and the Hussites had been crushed and silenced. Yet, Satan knew he had not won. In spite of the fact that the true Christians had been silenced, he knew there were still a lot of Christians who loved God and trusted in the grace of God through the blood of Jesus. He was just waiting with dread for the next preacher to start reading the Bible and proclaim God's Word. He did not have long to wait.

CHAPTER 7

THE REFORMATION
A Terrible Blow to Satan's Plan

At the beginning of the 16th century Satan's plan seemed to be going well. Satan had been able to so influence the Papacy and the priesthood that the people were kept in ignorance and fear. All the Bibles were now chained to the pulpits, and only the clergy were allowed to read them. The people did not have a proper understanding of the fear God, if they had it would have led them to hold Him in awe, worship and obey Him.

Instead, they pictured Jesus as a stern judge of whom they were afraid. The people looked to His mother Mary as the only way to find God's mercy. Under these circumstances, how could people love God? Since they had no confidence or joy in their salvation, how could they truly worship and praise God? Satan now had things in the church operating very much the way he desired.

The Pope had almost unlimited power over both the church and the civil government. This was true to such a degree that on May 5, 1514, the Papal orator declared, "There is an end of resistance to papal rule and religion. There is none to oppose. The whole body of Christendom is subject to its head" (the Pope).

As the Council of Lateran closed there were feasts, drinking of toasts and congratulatory speeches. Pope Leo received gifts and congratulations from many lands.

For 3½ years the world was reminded of what happens to those who oppose the Papacy. At the end of those 3½ years on October 31, 1517, a German by the name of Martin Luther nailed his ninety-five theses on the Cathedral door at Wittenberg, and the Reformation began.

Martin Luther was the son of peasants with a strict upbringing and a fine education. He was a university graduate and became a teacher at the University. He had great talents, both intellectually and musically, but he was tortured by his conscience. He knew that he had not kept God's law perfectly, and he was afraid of eternal damnation. For this reason, when he was traveling on the road during a thunderstorm and lightening was striking around him, he prayed to St. Ann and made a bargain. He vowed that if he would be spared from dying he would become a monk.

A few days later, on July 17, 1505, he entered the Augustinian monastery at Erfurt. His talents were quickly discovered; and in 1507 he entered the priesthood. A year later he became a teacher at the University of Wittenberg. He first taught philosophy but began to prepare himself to teach theology. He was called back to the monastery to teach there for a short time but in 1511 he returned to the University of Wittenberg.

It was at Wittenberg where he was teaching Romans and Galatians that he discovered the Bible passage in Galatians 3:11, *"The just shall live by faith"*. Suddenly his eyes were opened. He finally realized that he could not earn his way to heaven by being good or doing good works. Heaven was a free gift from God to those who believe in the finished work of the Lord Jesus Christ. There was now nothing that anyone could do for their salvation because Jesus had already shed his blood and made payment for the sins of the world. Once Luther realized this cardinal truth, the other false teachings of the Roman church such as; Penance, Purgatory, and praying to the Saints, began to fall off him like when a dog shakes off the water after a rain.

Satan and the Church of Rome would now find that they would have much more difficulty dealing with Luther then they had with John Huss. The German princes had been chaffing under the dictates of Rome. When Luther took a stand, they stood with him and protected him. When the Church of Rome condemned and conspired to kill him, Frederick the Wise had Luther disguised as a Knight and was hidden in a Castle. It was at that time, he translated the Bible into German.

There was a man in Switzerland by the name of Ulrich Zwingli. He began preaching against the superstitions in the Catholic Church a year before Luther nailed his 95 thesis to the castle door in Wittenberg. He became acquainted with Luther's writings in 1520 and they met together later. They agreed with each other on most things, but they disagreed concerning the Lord's Supper. Nevertheless both men started the fires of reformation which spread all over Europe.

Satan's plan was now in complete disarray. He wanted to keep the Church unified under the Pope in order to be able to better control it? Of course, the idea of the unity of the Church was nothing new. Jesus himself had prayed for the unity of the Church under Christ Himself, and led by the Holy Spirit. The idea of the Church under a papal head was Satanic.

Please understand. It is not the purpose of this book to come against the Roman Catholic Church. The very same things that happened in the Roman Catholic Church could happen in any Protestant church if it had a hierarchal system with the power of the state behind it. Whenever any man assumes the authority which belongs only to Christ and tries to coerce other men to do his bidding, he is assuming the role of God and is an easy prey to the deception of Satan.

Once reformation of the church began, it could not easily be stopped. For a while, it seemed like most of Europe might become Protestant. By 1540 all of North Germany had become Lutheran. Pope Paul III urged Emperor Charles V to go against the Protestants and offered him an army. The Pope declared the war a crusade and offered indulgences to all who would take part. The war lasted from 1546 to 1555, ending with the Peace of Augsburg, by which the Lutherans won legal recognition.

At about the time of Luther's death the Roman Catholic Church began the Counter Reformation. It was not intended to change the doctrines but to reform the wicked and immoral life of the clergy and to bring the Protestants back into the Catholic Church; if necessary by force. To carry this out, the Inquisition was used to hunt down the Protestant heretics. The accused heretics were subjected to the most horrible tortures to get them to deny their faith. They were then punished by fines, loss of property, exile, imprisonment, hanging, drowning, or burning. Many thousands lost their lives.

The Inquisition was so successful in Italy and Spain that these countries were soon rid of Protestantism. In other European countries, many were brought back into the Catholic Church.

In France, three savage wars were fought between the Catholics and Protestants (who were called Huguenots). These wars finally culminated in what is called, "The massacre of St.

Bartholomew." Several thousand Huguenots were tortured, mutilated, beheaded or otherwise put to death. The Pope ordered a medal struck in honor of the event.

Phillip II of Spain was a loyal son of the Roman Church and wanted to do all in his power to destroy Protestantism. Phillip thought that if he could conquer England, he could destroy Protestantism. He sent a Spanish fleet of 150 ships against England. The Spanish Armada contained larger and stronger ships than the English fleet, but the English ships were faster. In battle speed counts as well as strength.

The Spanish Armada set out on its journey on July 12, 1588. The fleet sailed into the English Channel in the form of a half moon which was seven miles from tip to tip. The small fast English ships did what they could against them and the Spanish Armada suffered losses. The armada then anchored their ships in Calais to get the help that was promised them by the Duke of Parma. While they were still anchored in the port, the English sent burning ships among the Spanish fleet. Panic stricken, the Spaniards put out to sea again as quickly as possible. Again the small English vessels pounced on them and sank some of their ships. When the Spaniards saw no hope of victory, they turned in flight to go around the north of Scotland and Ireland to return to Spain. On the way, they ran into a violent storm, and many of the ships were wrecked. Thousands of Spanish soldiers died. Only 53 vessels returned to Spain. The Spanish Armada failed, and England remained Protestant.

Even though Emperor Charles V signed the peace of Augsburg in 1555, the Jesuits were not satisfied to let matters rest there. They stirred up hatred against the Lutherans and persuaded Emperor Ferdinand to go to war against them in

Bohemia. This was the beginning of The Thirty Years' War which spread throughout all of Europe.

The battle had been going against the Protestants until Gustavus Adolphus, King of Sweden, entered the battle. Even though Gustavus was struck down by a bullet, his army went on to defeat the Catholic army in 1632. The war however continued on for 16 more years until peace was finally made in 1648.

In the peace of Westphalia both the Lutheran and the Reformed churches were granted religious liberty. Most of southern Europe, Germany, and Switzerland were Catholic, while northern Europe remained Protestant.

This had been one of the most destructive wars in history. In Germany alone, the population was reduced from 15 million to less than 5 million by the time the war was over. The destruction was less in other countries, but it was still considerable.

The Catholic Church was still as corrupt as ever, and the Protestant churches had lost many of their pastors. In many churches the preaching and teaching of God's word was neglected. The Church needed to be restored.

There was division among the pastors as how to best restore the church. Some felt that pure doctrine was the most important. Others said the people need to learn to live a life of holiness. Others made human reason their top priority.

Certainly Satan enjoyed all the blood, gore, and confusion in the churches; but he knew that he had suffered a terrible defeat. There was just no way force could be used to bring the church back under the Papacy. Satan had been planning for this contingency, and already the Conspiracy was progressing in other areas. Satan's plans had not changed. Only his strategy would change.

CHAPTER 8

ROOTS OF THE MODERN CONSPIRACY

The modern day satanic conspiracy might be compared with the fabled blind men and the elephant. The story is told of six blind men who went to see an elephant. All of them were blind, but thought they might gain understanding of the elephant by feeling the animal. One happened to fall against the elephant's side and described the elephant as a wall. The second man felt of the tusk and said the elephant was like a spear. The third man grabbed the trunk and thought the elephant was like a snake. The fourth man put his arms around a leg and proclaimed the elephant was like a tree. The fifth man felt of an ear and said the elephant was like a giant fan. The sixth man grabbed hold of the tail and thought he had a rope.

There have been many books written on the modern conspiracy. One man says the conspiracy arises out of international banking; another that it is the outgrowth of the Illuminati; while other people describe it as Free Masonry, the Occult, Humanism, Secularism, Communism, Islam, or the New World Order.

Like the blind men they are all correct to a degree. The modern satanic conspiracy is all of these things. The Satanic Conspiracy can be broken down into four divisions;

the **Philosophical**, the **Political**, the **Monetary** and the **Religious**.

The roots of this conspiracy grew out of the changing conditions in Europe and the world. In the early 1300's a new kind of thinking began in Italy and then spread into all of Europe. This new kind of thinking is known as the Renaissance. The name Renaissance comes from a Latin word which means to be reborn. Many European scholars and artists began to study the arts and ancient wisdom of Greece and Rome. They wanted to recapture the spirit of the Greek and Roman cultures. In medieval times people thought that a person's main responsibility was to pray to God and to seek the salvation of one's soul. Renaissance thinkers emphasized a person's responsibility and duty to society.

The changes brought about by the Renaissance happened very gradually and did not immediately affect most Europeans, but in future generations these ideas greatly influenced the whole fabric of society.

The Renaissance thinkers believed that people should understand and appreciate the cultures of ancient Greece and Rome in order to better know how to conduct their own lives. In order to understand the laws and customs of Greece and Rome, it was necessary to learn the ancient Greek and Roman languages. They searched through monasteries and libraries throughout Europe for long neglected manuscripts of classical authors. They were greatly aided in their search for understanding by the invention of the printing press with movable type in the 1450's. The fall of Constantinople to Islam in 1453 also aided the Renaissance.

Constantinople had been the capital of the Eastern Roman Empire and the head of the Greek Orthodox Church.

It had great universities and was a repository of Greek learning, literature, and culture from ancient times. When Constantinople fell, there was a migration of university professors and scholars who fled to the West and brought as many books with them as they possibly could.

The Renaissance provided many benefits for mankind. Art was now softened, humanized, and beautified. The knowledge of literature and education was greatly increased. History now took on a greater significance. Architecture began to take on the beauty of the ancient world. Advancements in science took place because inquiring minds wanted a better understanding of the physical universe. A better understanding of astronomy, mathematics, and navigation helped Christopher Columbus to discover America.

PHILOSOPHICAL AND RELIGIOUS ROOTS

In the last chapter we looked at some of the religious roots during the 16th and 17th centuries. The things that were happening in the church were influenced by the Renaissance, the invention of the printing press, the fall of Constantinople, the revival of Greek and Latin, and by the discovery of America.

Satan doesn't have the power to control everything or to make things happen the way he wants, but he does have the intelligence and the experience to take advantage of what is happening. In this chapter we will see how Satan tries to influence the things that are happening in such a way as to gain control of mankind and to set up the whole world in rebellion against God.

In the area of religion and political science, the Renaissance was a mixed blessing. In medieval thinking everything centered on God. Now man was coming back into the picture. Without question, man's welfare and social relationships are important. People should have a proper concern for the welfare of mankind and society in general

It is important that man also has a proper relationship with God. He needs to know and understand how much God really loves him and how God desires the welfare of all mankind. Unfortunately, Renaissance thinking went too far and **humanism** was too often the result. **Humanism** takes God out of the center and replaces him with man. When man becomes the center, there is no longer a place for God. We will discuss Humanism more in a later chapter.

Renaissance thinking eventually lead to **rationalism**. This time period was also known as the **Age of Reason** during the 16 and 1700's. The philosophers of the Age of Reason emphasized the use of reason as the best method of learning truth. They relied heavily on the scientific method and experimentation. Using this method, great advances were made in the scientific field. They accepted the principle that reason was the supreme authority in matters of opinion, belief, and conduct. In this, they went too far. Reason combined with patient observation and experimentation reveals much truth, but that is not the only source of truth. Unfortunately, they rejected many truths of the Bible. The only truth they would accept was what seemed reasonable to them. Most of them believed that God created the world but then left it strictly alone to run by itself. This theory rules out the possibility of miracles or any other special acts of God. They liked to think of the universe as a clock that keeps perfect time because it was designed by a superior clockmaker.

In France, these philosophers concerned themselves with unjust social and political conditions. The result was the French Revolution. In England John Locke believed that people must unite and form a state in order to protect their lives, liberty, and property. The writings of John Locke greatly influenced the leaders of the American Revolution.

Toward the end of the 18th century, a revolt against the ideal of reason began to take place. Feeling began to be considered more important than reason for many people. Extending from about 1789 until 1837, the **romantic age** stressed emotion and passion over reason. For many people the obsession with reason seemed too artificial. **Romantics** wanted freedom for the individual and they rejected all restraints.

When we look back at these various philosophies, we realize that there is truth in all of them; but all of them are lacking. None of them give full satisfaction. According to Renaissance thinkers, the good life is achieved through knowledge and understanding. In the Age of reason, they thought the good life was achieved by rational thinking. The romantics thought that feeling and emotion was the most important thing.

In order to achieve the good life one must have more than knowledge, understanding, rational thought, and emotions. Without God, our lives are empty and we can never receive full satisfaction. Satan was well aware of this and was quite ready to take advantage of it.

When all of these philosophies fail what's left? The answer is Nihilism. Nihilism is formed from part of the Latin word **nihil**, which means nothing. **Nihilism** is an extreme form of skepticism which denies that it is even possible to know the truth. For a nihilist, there is no good or evil, right or wrong. A nihilist ignores all restraints of conscience and feels free to do anything he wants as long as he thinks he can get by with it. Satan wasn't able to make the people think and do all the things they did. He did, however, know how to take advantage of these philosophies. He would guide them along in order to set the world up for the final modern-day Conspiracy.

MONETARY AND POLITICAL ROOTS

Money and politics have always gone together. Governments need money in order to operate. They obtain money by taxing, borrowing, or by cheapening the money supply. This has been true throughout history, and it has never been more true than today. Before we get into the inner workings of money in politics, we need to see what money is.

WHAT IS MONEY?

Throughout history, real money has always been a medium of exchange which also has certain characteristics. First of all it has to have real value which is recognized by most people. Second, it has to be portable, (something that you can carry around with you). Third, it has to be something that is scarce and cannot be counterfeited.

There have been times when people have used commodities for money. In the United States during the colonial period, people used tobacco for money, because gold and silver was scarce and tobacco was useful in trade. Using commodities for money, however, is not an efficient way to trade. Think about trying to lug a bushel of wheat to the store in order to buy some eggs, meat or vegetables. No, money must be something that you can carry in your pocket and which has real value. Throughout history gold, silver, and copper have best served that purpose

GOVERNMENT AND MONEY

Government and money are inseparable because government cannot operate without money. Civil servants, judges, police, and administrators must be paid. So where is government going to get the money? The money comes from the people, of course. It has been said that are only two things are certain -- death and taxes. Historically, one of the first things governments have usually done is to standardize money by weighing out a certain amount of gold, silver, or copper and then putting the official government stamp upon that coin.

By providing a standardized coin for the citizens to use in commerce, the economy begins to flourish. Everything goes along fine until the rulers decide to get greedy. They want to live in fine palaces and work in fancy buildings. They build roads and various public works which makes life better for everybody, but all of these things cost money and taxes have to be raised. Then one day the government decides that it needs to declare war. For our purpose, it doesn't matter whether the war is a good idea or not. In either case, wars are expensive and the government needs a lot of money.

We mentioned before that there are three places for the government to get it. It can increase taxes, but let us assume the citizens are already paying all they can afford to pay. In a case like this the government can do what governments have always done, it can cheapen the money. How do you cheapen the money? You take the coin and chop off part of the outside so you have a smaller coin but tell the people that they must accept the new coin as having the same value. What happened of course was that people hid the old coins and used the new coins in commerce. So now the government decided upon a new tactic. They would mix base metals like copper and nickel with their gold and silver. That way they would be able to increase the number of coins with their present supply of gold and silver. Unfortunately, as the number of coins increased, they began to buy less and less. Nevertheless, the wars were fought and the people were impoverished more and more.

Any time you increase the money supply without increasing the amount of products to buy, you will soon find that it takes more money to buy the same amount of goods. If you double the money supply, very soon real goods and services will cost twice as much.

Watering down or cheapening the money supply is bad, but things really went from bad to worse when the bankers got involved.

BANKING

Banking started with the money changers in the temples and markets. When people from far away came to worship at the temple or buy things at the local market, they brought their own money with them. In order to buy things in the city where they were, they needed to use a local currency. Therefore, they had to exchange their money for the local money. The money changers were very happy to oblige. Of course, they kept some of the money for themselves as could be expected. They had to make a living. They were also exposed to considerable risk; both to themselves and to their money by having it in a public place.

Of course, the money that they used to exchange had to be kept in a safe place. They had the safest depositories around and they kept a little extra for lending. They charged interest for their loans, and this also increased their income. Since the money-changers/bankers had the strongest safe around, merchants and others, who had money brought their gold and silver to the bank. The banker then wrote them a scrip or deposit slip which stated that they had deposited gold or silver with the bank. The bankers note promised to fully refund the deposited amount of gold or silver upon demand. The banker was also happy to pay the depositors a little interest on their deposits.

After a while people began to trust the banker. Every time they wanted their gold or silver the banker was happy to get it for them, so the people began to feel that their deposits were safe. The depositors were told that their deposit slip was as good as gold, and after a while they began to believe it. They also found that it was much easier to carry around pieces of paper than it was gold or silver, which was heavy and people began to use the scrip to buy things just as if it was real money, instead of just a promise to pay.

Very soon the bankers discovered that people liked using pieces of paper with which to trade. While the depositors could demand their gold or silver at any time, they seldom did so. Even when people came to borrow money from the bank, they were most often content with a deposit slip which was just as good as gold. Since people let their gold stay in the bank, the banker could loan out more money than he actually had on deposit. So the bankers began to loan out as much as twenty times what they had on deposit by writing scrip. As long as people had confidence in the banker, everything would be fine. If people began to loose confidence in the bank or the banker, they would want their money back. If everyone wanted their money at the same time, the banker would be in big trouble.

Even if the bank never had any problem with depositors wanting their money back, there was still a big problem. The bankers were creating inflation by multiplying the money supply without increasing the supply of goods that money could buy.

BANKING AND GOVERNMENT:

Whenever governments get into trouble, the bankers are always ready to help. Perhaps a government wants to reward its supporters or make war against its neighbor. This will take money. Mr. Banker is always ready to help. He says don't debase your coins; I will lend you the money.

Now why would the banker want to lend the government money? Lending money to governments is the way a banker can become even richer and gain control of the government. The Bible says that the borrower is servant to the lender. This is true, and it doesn't matter whether it is an individual or a government.

Here is the way it works. You make a $100.00 deposit in your bank. The bank is very happy to pay you 2% which equals $2.00 per year. The bank then loans out 90% of it at 6%. The person borrowing the money owes the bank $90.00, which the bank considers part of its assets and in turn lends 90% of this $90.00. This continues until the bank has loaned out $500.00 from the original $100.00 you deposited. *(Actually they often loaned out far more than 5 times the amount that was deposited.)* Let's see how this works out. The bank pays you $2.00 interest on your deposit and it collects interest on the $500.00 that it loaned out, as a result of your deposit. It has charged 6% interest on the $500.00 therefore the bank has taken in $30.00 interest but has only paid out $2.00 interest.

It is also interesting to note that banks only lend out enough money to pay back the original loan. In order to pay the interest one must borrow it, take it out of savings, profit from operations, or otherwise take the money out of circulation. Through the repayment of loans and interest, it would not take long for all the gold, silver and paper money to end up in the banker's vault. That is the reason banks have to continually increase the money supply. If only precious metals are used as money, then it is impossible to multiply the money supply. If you are using paper money, all you have to do is start the printing press.

(Note: Since 1900 AD money supply in the United States has been expanded. It now takes a dollar today to buy what two cents used to.)

BANKING AND WAR

Fighting wars requires a huge amount of money and that is where the banks come in. Huge international banking cartels have been lending to governments for the last several hundred years. They usually lend to both sides in the wars they help to instigate. It really isn't so much about making money as it is in being able to pull the levers of power. If a government doesn't want to cooperate with them, they let it be known that money can be lent to their enemy. In the following chapters we will see how the International Banks have fomented revolutions and set nations against each other for the express purpose of wielding power. Power is sought not only to satisfy their own ambitions, but also to satisfy the dictates of their master, Satan.

A WORD ABOUT BANKING:

One might easily get the impression that I think all bankers are evil. Actually, I have two daughters who used to work for banks, and I do not consider them to be evil. You cannot classify all bankers as being evil anymore than you can classify all politicians, lawyers or schoolteachers as evil.

The Bible does have a lot to say about money, banking and interest. In Old Testament times, God forbid the Israelites to charge each other interest on anything that was borrowed. Jesus talked a great deal about money and our attitudes toward it. The apostle Paul did not say that money was the root of all evil but that the love of money was the root of all evil. In the following chapters we will be talking about how the love of money and the power that it buys can be very evil indeed.

DIFFERENT KINDS OF BANKS

There are different kinds of banks. First, there are the local consumer type banks. These are where most people put their deposits and do their checking. These banks also make loans for mortgages, cars, consumer goods, and small business loans.

The next kind of banks we might label as commercial banks. The commercial banks do most of their business with large corporations. They also buy mortgages and other financial papers from smaller banks.

The last types of banks with which we will deal are the international banks. The International banks lend to governments and other smaller banks. The central banks of various countries are also part of the international banking community. This is the type of bank we are usually referring to when we speak of banks.

THE BEGINNING OF INTERNATIONAL BANKING

As strange as it may seem, international banking was started by the Knights Templar in the Catholic Church. They were a military order which began during the time of the Crusades. They had extensive land holdings all across Europe. It was their practice to sell a person a demand note in one location and let him redeem it at any of their other castles. This enabled people to move their money across Europe without the risk of being robbed.

Some years later other banking families followed the same procedure. Most notably were the Rothschild family banks.

THE ROTHSCHILD FAMILY BANKS

The Rothschild name is intimately connected with international banking. The name Rothschild means red shield which also appears on their coat of arms. It all started with Mayer Amschel Rothschild (1744-1812). Rothschild, however, was not his original name. His original name was Bauer. He was the son of a Jewish merchant in Frankfurt, Germany, by the name of Moses Amschel Bauer who was in the money lending business. Moses Bauer placed a red hexagram above the entrance door to his counting house.

In 1760 Mayer Amschel Bauer went to work for a bank owned by the Oppenheimer family in Hanover, Germany He was very successful and soon became a junior partner.

While working at the bank he becomes acquainted with General von Estorff.

After his father died, he returned to Frankfort to take over his father's business. He recognized the significance of the red hexagram and changed his name from Bauer to Rothschild. The word Rothschild means red sign. ("Rot," is German for, "Red," and "Schild," is German for "Sign.") (During the middle ages the Jews in Europe adopted the hexagram as a Jewish symbol and called it the Star of David.

After Mayer Amschel Rothschild opened his bank in Frankfort, he discovered that General von Estorff was now attached to the court of Prince William IX of Hesse-Hanau, one of the richest royal houses in Europe. Mayer Rothschild then contacted the General on the pretext of selling him valuable coins and trinkets at discounted prices. As he had planned, he was then introduced to Prince William who was also pleased to buy coins and trinkets at greatly discounted prices. Rothschild then offered the prince a bonus for any other business the Prince can direct his way.

In this way, Rothschild became a close associate with Prince William and received permission to hang a sign on the front of his business declaring that he is, "M. A. Rothschild, by appointment court factor to his highness, Prince William of Hanau."

In the meantime, Mayer Amschel Rothschild had been greatly increasing his wealth by making profitable investments for several of the royal families of Europe. He began installing his sons in the family business when they were 12 years old. He soon developed a banking empire by installing his five sons in various banks he set up in strategic cities all over Europe. Salomon Mayer he sent to Vienna, Nathan Mayer to London,

Calnann Mayer to Naples, and James Mayer to Paris. He kept his oldest son Amschel Mayer, in Frankfurt. Now he was in a position to affect money and interest throughout Europe.

They became incredibly wealthy by financing governments to fight one another. Since the Rothschild family was scattered all over Europe, they could easily finance both sides of the warring parties from one of their branch banks. In this way they were able to pull the strings of power throughout Europe. They didn't worry about the losing side being able to pay the money back. They were always able to increase their wealth through compound interest. What they really wanted was power.

During the Napoleonic Wars in the early 1800's the Rothschild family was heavily invested in the British war effort. They handled the shipment of gold to the British army in Portugal and Spain, as well as arranging the payments to their Continental allies. Through the commissions earned on these transactions, the Rothschild wealth began to grow.

The Rothschild's biggest fortune was made however, when Napoleon lost to the British at Waterloo on June 18, 1815. It happened like this. The Rothschild family had set up a European wide network of carrier pigeon stations. They used the pigeons to send information to one another about anything that might affect their investments or banking business. They soon gained a reputation for being first with the news.

When the British won the battle at Waterloo, a carrier pigeon was immediately sent to Nathan Rothschild in London. Nathan immediately went to the stock exchange and began selling stocks. When other investors saw Nathan doing this, they concluded that Napoleon must have won.

Therefore they began to dump their stocks on the market in a panic sellout. After the prices crashed, Nathan began to buy everything in sight. At the end of the day, Nathan Rothschild practically owned Great Britain.

"Permit me to issue and control the money of a nation and I care not who makes the laws." -- Mayer Amschel Rothschild, founder of the Rothschild banking dynasty, 1790

In the following chapters we will see how the banking interests play out in the Modern Conspiracy, but for now we need to go back a few years to 1776.

CHAPTER 9

1776 THE BEGINNING OF THE MODERN CONSPIRACY

We all have certain dates that are very important to us, like our birthday or anniversary. Nations also have certain dates which are not easily forgotten, like 9/11 and December 7, 1941. There are some historical dates which have an influence that goes far beyond an individual or nation. A few dates are significant to all people; such as the birth of Christ, the fall of Rome, the beginning of Islam, and the Reformation of the Church. The year 1776 has that kind of significance. Three events occurred that year which has affected the lives of almost everyone. Two of those events are celebrated every year, while the other event is less well known.

The date that no doubt comes to all my American readers is July 4, 1776. It is a day of fireworks and hotdogs. It is the day that the Declaration of Independence was signed. It is considered the birthday of the United States.

The second date we need to consider is May 1st, often called May Day. Throughout history it has been a celebration of the season of Spring. It is also a neo-pagan feast day, Saint Mary's day, and a day for organized labor. In many countries, May 1st is a national holiday, but that is not the reason we bring this day to your attention.

On May 1, 1776, Adam Weishaupt officially completed the organization of the Illuminati. While the Illuminati supposedly only lasted a few years, the conspiratorial teaching, planning, and directives went under-ground. It has been affecting the whole human race ever since. We will go into more detail later in this chapter.

The third date in 1776 that we need to make note of is the year that Adam Smith published his book on the economy. It is called "The Wealth of Nations." In this book Smith lays out the basic theory and principals of private property, capital investment, wages, prices and the free enterprise system. The United States has been the country which has most closely followed the principals set forth by Smith. This is one of the reasons the United States became the freest and most wealthy country in the world during the 19th and 20th centuries. Unfortunately, the United States is now losing its place in the world.

I would like to get back to July 4, 1776 and the founding of the United States. First though, it is necessary to see what the influence of international banking and the international conspiracy has had upon this nation from the very beginning.

THE ILLUMINATI OR LUCIFERIAN CONSPIRACY

It all started with Adam Weishaupt about 1770. Adam Weishaupt had a very interesting history. Even though he was a Jew, he converted to Roman Catholicism and became a Jesuit-trained professor of Cannon law. As a professor of Cannon law, he taught at Engelstock University until he defected from Christianity to follow Satan. He then began his writings for the establishment of the **Illuminati** or the **Luciferian Conspiracy**.

Some people have thought that Mayer Amschel Rothschild financed him. That seems unlikely, because at that time Rothschild had not yet come into his wealth. In the 1770's, Rothschild was a moderately successful antique coin dealer and stock broker; but he had nowhere near the wealth of his contemporary Jewish bankers. While Adam Weishaupt and Rothschild were both **Ashkenazi Jews,** there is no indication that they knew one another at that time. It is more likely that Weishaupt was financed by Moses Mendelssohn and other Jewish bankers.

> Ashkenazi Jews were not actually Jews according to their blood line. They originated from a country called Khazaria which was located between the Black and Caspian Seas. In 740 A.D. all the people of Khazaria under orders from their king converted to Judaism. The Jews who actually descended from the nation of Israel were known as Shephardim Jews.

Regardless as to how he was financed, it was in 1770 that Weishaupt began to write the master plan of Satan. Adam Weishaupt called his organization **The Illuminati.** This name was chosen because the name of Satan is Lucifer. The meaning of the name Lucifer is the bearer of light; therefore, those who embrace these satanic teachings have become illuminated. Weishaupt edited both Jewish and Jesuit materials which he included in his master plan. He completed his work on May 1, 1776. (Communist and Socialist nations continue to celebrate May 1st in honor of this great event.)

Weishaupt laid out a plan for the Illuminati to take over all the countries of the world. They would be ruled by a few elite men as directed by Satan. In order to accomplish this they would train and educate their agents to infiltrate all levels of government to carry out the secret plans of their masters.

The main features of the Illuminati plan were to:

1. Gain control of men already in high places by bribing them with money and sex. They were to be kept in bondage by blackmail, threats of financial ruin, public exposure, and physical harm.

2. Gain control of education. First they would get their agents teaching on the faculties of colleges and universities where they could cultivate students for high government assignments. After they had been selected they would be sent off for special training, like the Rhodes scholarships of today.

3. All influential people trapped by the Illuminati and the students who had been specially educated and trained, were to be used as agents. They were to be placed behind the scenes in all governments as experts and specialists. They would advise the top executives to adopt policies which would serve the Illuminati. Their purpose was to bring about the destruction of the governments and religions they were elected or appointed to serve.

4. They were to gain absolute control over the press. All news and information could then be slanted to convince the masses that a one world government is the only solution for the problems of the world.

In order to carry out his plan to rule over all the countries of the world, Weishaupt ordered the Illuminati to cause strife and unrest in various countries. He especially had his eye on France and Great Britain, because they were the two greatest world powers at that time. It was his plan to start the French Revolution in 1789, but an act of God got in his way.

In 1784, Weishaupt had issued his orders to the Illuminates in France for the French Revolution. He had a German writer named Zwack put these orders into book form which contained the entire Illuminati plan. A copy of this book was being sent to Illuminates in France when the carrier was struck by lightening and killed as he rode on his way from Germany to France. The police found the subversive documents on his body and turned them over to the proper authorities.

After a careful study of the plot, the Bavarian Government was convinced that the documents were genuine. These documents showed how the Illuminati planned to use wars and revolutions in order to bring about a centralized world government under their control.

In 1785, the Bavarian Government outlawed the Illuminati, and closed the lodges of the Grand Orient. In 1786, they published all the details of the conspiracy, the English title of that publication being "The Original Writings of the Order and Sect of the Illuminati". Copies of the entire conspiracy were sent to all the heads of Church and State in Europe. Unfortunately, this warning was ignored. Since the Illuminati had now been exposed, they decided to pretend to disband. What they actually did was to go underground.

Weishaupt ordered his followers to infiltrate into the lodges of Blue Masonry, and form their own secret societies within these secret societies. Only Masons who had an internationalist's outlook and who had rejected God were to be initiated into the Illuminati.

In order to infiltrate into Masonic Lodges in Britain, Weishaupt invited John Robison over to Europe. Robison was a high degree Mason in the Scottish rite. He was a professor of natural philosophy at Edinburgh University and secretary of The Royal Society of Edinburgh. Robison did not fall for the lie that the objective of the Illuminati was to create a benevolent dictatorship, but he kept his reaction to himself so well he was entrusted with a copy of Weishaupt's revised conspiracy for study and safekeeping.

Because the warnings about the Illuminati were ignored, the French Revolution broke out in 1789, as scheduled by Weishaupt.

In order to alert other governments to their danger, Robison published, in 1789, a book entitled "Proof of a Conspiracy to Destroy All Governments and Religions", but his warnings were also ignored.

The men who had directed the French Revolution decided to use Napoleon Bonaparte to topple several more of the Crowned Heads of Europe. That, however, didn't work out the way it was planned.

One more thing needs to be said about the Illuminati at this time. While Weishaupt was the one who actually did the writing and organizing of the Illuminati, he did not act alone. He was a front for the international bankers who financed and directed him. These bankers were in turn agents of Satan. This was and still is Satan's plan - to gain control of the earth.

Satan's plan for France worked, but he didn't succeed in gaining the control he wished for rest of Europe and certainly not Great Brittan.

CHAPTER 10

1776 THE BIRTHDAY OF THE UNITED STATES

J uly 4, 1776 rightly is considered the birth of the United States. On that date the signing of the Declaration of Independence from England took place. The birth of any baby requires a mother. Without question the mother of the United States is England. The circumstances of this birth began almost 200 years earlier back in England. While it is a part of Europe it is separated by water from the rest of Europe and developed a little differently. The people in England were more independent than most Europeans and objected to the idea of the **"Divine Right of Kings."**

THE DIVINE RIGHT OF KINGS:

The kings of Europe exercised the divine right of kings. They claimed that their right to rule came directly from God. Therefore, anything they said or did could not be challenged. The Kings of England also tried to do the same thing, but the English people objected. In 1215 AD, the English barons met with King John to draw up documents which limited some of his rights as King. He was forced to accept the fact that his will could be bound by law. This document was called the Magna Carta, which means great paper. It also established certain rights for his subjects, such as habeas corpus which guarded against unlawful imprisonment. It also dealt with rights to private property, inheritance, taxation and many other issues which burdened the people.

The Magna Carta may very well be called the beginning of constitutional law. It influenced common-law in England and in the United States. Some of the things written in the Magna Carta are found in the Constitution of the United States and in the Bill of Rights.

JOHN LOCKE (1632-1704)

Locke was an English philosopher who wrote two treatises of government. In the first treatise he took aim against the divine right of kings. He claimed that neither scripture nor reason supported it. In his second treatise he discussed natural rights which an individual had before government came into being. He argued that we have a right of survival. In order to survive; he claimed we must have rights to life, liberty, health and property.

He claimed that the proper use for government is to help us survive. Some things individuals find that they are not able to do alone, such as maintain law and order, fight wars, and build roads and bridges. It is proper therefore to voluntarily transfer some rights to government to do collectively what an individual might find difficult or impossible to do for himself. The purpose however is to help the individual to survive and prosper. Locke claimed that the only legitimate government is by the consent of those governed. Any government that rules without the consent of the people is not legitimate; therefore in theory at least, they can and perhaps should be overthrown.

The aim of such a legitimate civil government should be to preserve the rights to life, liberty, health, and property of its citizens; and to prosecute and punish those who violate the rights of others.

Locke also argued that more religious groups actually helped to prevent civil unrest. He argued that civil unrest resulted from the attempt to prevent different religions from being practiced, rather than tolerating their proliferation.

3. RELIGIOUS TOLERATION

There was no religious tolerance in England. Before the Reformation, England, as well as the rest of Europe was Catholic. When King Henry VIII came to power, he had a succession of six wives. In 1534, Henry wanted the Pope to annul his marriage to Catherine of Aragon, but the Pope refused. King Henry therefore decided that he would become head of his own church. He broke ties with Rome and started the Church of England. After King Henry died, his son Edward VI began to rule. He was only 10 years old. During his rule the Catholics were persecuted.

In 1553, Mary became Queen. She was a devout Catholic and persecuted the Protestants. She is noted for burning 274 Protestants at the stake.

In 1558, Elizabeth became Queen. Queen Elizabeth has been considered by history to have been a very wise and moderate ruler. While she set out to more firmly establish the Church of England, she also had a great deal of success in balancing the interests of both the Puritans and die-hard Catholics. Toward the end of her reign, however, she began to punish those who would not conform to the Church of England.

When King James I came to power in 1603, he was especially harsh toward all those who would not conform to the Church of England. It was under his reign in 1611, that the King James Bible was translated.

4. RELIGIOUS FREEDOM

In the 1380's, John Wycliffe produced the first hand-written English language translation of the Bible. With the help of his followers, and many faithful scribes, Wycliffe produced dozens of English language manuscript copies of the Scriptures. Wycliffe was well-known throughout Europe for his opposition to the teaching of the organized church, which he believed to be contrary to the Bible.

The second step toward religious freedom occurred with the Puritans of the 16th and 17th Centuries. A Puritan was anyone seeking purity of worship and doctrine. King Henry VIII had rejected the Pope of Rome, but in effect had made himself Pope. There had been some stirrings toward reform but it had not gone far enough. During the reign of Queen Mary I, (also called bloody Mary), the Protestants were so persecuted that many of them went to Europe. There they came in contact with Calvinist and Lutheran teachings. Some of these people eventually came back to England. Under the persecution of King Charles I, they then immigrated to America.

COLONIZATION OF THE NEW WORLD

In 1587, Sir Walter Raleigh was commissioned by Queen Elizabeth to establish a Colony in the New World. They landed on Roanoke Island, North Carolina, where the first child to English parents was born in America. They named her Virginia

Dare. The ships returned to England for more supplies. They were delayed getting back because Spain had sent a fleet of ships against England. They were not able to return to the colony until after the Spanish Armada was defeated by storms and the British navy. When they finally returned to the colony in 1590, the whole colony had disappeared.

In 1607, a colony was set up in Jamestown, Virginia. They came for gold but didn't find any and the people who came were ill equipped to survive in the new world.

The colonies who settled in New England were quite different. They came so they might be free to worship God in their own way.

In 1620, the Puritans first went to Holland and then to America. They established the Plymouth Colony in Massachusetts.

When King Charles I came to power in England, he was not only religiously intolerant, but also decided he would exercise absolute rule. He decided that he would not give the people any part in government. As a result, in 1630, 20,000 people left England for America.

In 1634, Maryland was settled by Catholics who wanted to be able to worship as they pleased. They also exercised a great deal of toleration to people of other religions who settled there.

GOD'S PLAN

God's plan for the United States of America was one of blessing. He wanted a people that would honor him and spread his message of grace to the rest of the world. He wanted to call the people of that land His people; and He wanted them to live in peace and prosperity. Indeed, this land has been blessed. Many times though, people have missed out on the God's blessing because they have not acknowledged and served Him, as they should have.

Those who first settled America acknowledged God and felt they had a mission to proclaim God's word to the Indians. Even the first permanent English settlement at Jamestown felt that God had a higher purpose in their undertaking.

Robert Hunt was Chaplain of the expedition that founded the colony at Jamestown, Virginia. Right after they landed he led a Service of worship, praise, and thanksgiving. He dedicated this land to the glory of God and the extension of His Kingdom. Then he planted a cross at Cape Henry, which they had named after the Prince of Wales.

The colonies that came later, such as the Puritans in New England and the Catholics in Maryland were even more religiously based. Their whole purpose in coming to the new world was founded on divine principals, religious freedom, and missionary zeal.

SATAN'S PLAN

Satan's plan was to frustrate and destroy anything good that might occur in the New World. He sought to do whatever he could to stir up strife with the Indians and squabbles among the colonists.

Not long after the colony was established at Jamestown and the colony began to prosper, Satan brought slavery to the New World. In 1619, a Dutch slave trader exchanged his cargo of Africans for food. These Africans became indentured servants. Indentured servants were not what we generally think of as slaves. They were people who owed a debt and had traded their freedom for a time in order to pay off a debt. In this, they were in a similar legal position of many poor Englishmen who traded several years of labor in exchange for passage to America.

The idea of a race-based slave system did not fully develop until the 1680's. By the 1750's though, slavery had become firmly established; especially in Maryland, Virginia, and South Carolina. Of course slavery is wrong, and Satan would make sure that Americans would pay dearly for it.

MOVING TOWARD INDEPENDENCE

The French began to settle in Canada and then ventured through the Ohio valley on down to Louisiana. It was inevitable that there would eventually be clashes with the English settlers in the colonies who were also migrating toward the West. After several such clashes, delegates from New England, New York, Pennsylvania, and Maryland met together and made a treaty with the Iroquois Indians. They also decided that a union of the colonies was absolutely necessary for security and defense. Benjamin Franklin submitted a plan for union, but it was not adopted at that time.

These clashes continued until England formally declared war with France in 1756. What is known as the French and Indian War was fought in earnest on the American continent until 1759. The war continued in Europe until 1763. In the peace treaty which followed, France surrendered all of her possessions on the continent east of the Mississippi, except New Orleans. The way was now open for the Colonies to expand westward.

TENSION BETWEEN ENGLAND AND THE COLONIES

During the struggle with France, England's national debt was doubled. Since the Colonies were considered the greatest beneficiaries of the war, England wanted the colonies to help pay for it. That sounds fair enough but unfortunately, at that time England had a very clever but stupid king. King George III packed the parliament with his friends that would do what he wanted them to, and they did some very stupid things.

1. They began to enforce the trade laws. The trade laws had been in existence for some time but had not been enforced. These laws required that trade had to be done with British ships and shipped to and from British ports. In this way British merchants could skim the cream off of all transactions. This made trade far more expensive for the colonies. These laws were also intended to keep the colonies as producers of commodities, with England being the supplier of all manufactured goods. Most manufacturing in the colonies was forbidden for that reason.

2. England thought they needed to keep a standing army in America to guard against Indian attack and to prevent the French from returning. Of course they wanted the Americans to pay for it

3. In 1765, Parliament passed the Stamp Act. This was not well received in America. The colonists resolved to resist this tax and not to give up the right to tax themselves. This idea, the English people had asserted ever since

the Magna Charta in 1215; that no people should be taxed except by themselves or their representatives. This right was held dear by the colonists. The Stamp Tax was unenforceable and repealed in 1766, but in 1767 the Townshend Acts were passed. This merely tried to accomplish the same thing with a new twist. This was not acceptable either. It was finally repealed except for the Tea Tax. The American response was to have a Boston Tea Party whereby some of the colonists disguised themselves like Indians, boarded a ship with the tea, and threw the tea into the sea.

4. British judges and governors were made independent of colonial assemblies.
5. The protection of the rights to a trail by jury was in some cases taken away.

These things were bad enough but the worst was yet to come.

THE INTOLERABLE ACTS OF PARLIAMENT

1. **The Boston Port Bill.** This bill closed the port of Boston, allowing no ships to come or go until the tea which had been destroyed was paid for. An English man-of-war was sent to blockade the port.
2. **The Massachusetts Act.** This bill revoked the Massachusetts charter of 1691, and a new form of government was instituted. The upper house was now to be appointed by the crown,

and the governor's power was increased. He no longer had to answer to the people. Judges, magistrates, and sheriffs were to be appointed by the royal governor and would no longer be elected. The right to hold a public meeting was abolished, and such meetings were to be broken up.

3. **The Quartering Act.** Under this act in 1774, General Gage was made governor of Massachusetts and more troops were to be quartered in Boston.

THE FIRST CONTINENTAL CONGRESS 1774

These acts were directed at Massachusetts, but they threatened the rights of all the other colonies. Provisions were sent to Boston from the other colonies. Virginia appointed a day for prayer and fasting. Patrick Henry and Thomas Jefferson had already secured from the Burgesses in Virginia a permanent *Committee of Correspondence, "to maintain a correspondence with our sister colonies".* Other colonies followed this example. Because of the way that the English Parliament was treating the colonies, the suggestion was made for a congress of the colonies. Massachusetts issued the call, and the congress met at Philadelphia, September 5, 1774. There were delegates from every colony except Georgia. The governor of Georgia prevented any delegates from Georgia to attend.

The Congress published a "Declaration of Rights" in which it demanded the repeal of the coercive measures against Massachusetts, denounced as illegal a standing army in time of peace without the consent of the colony, and complained about the dissolution of their assemblies. The colonies denied the right of Parliament to legislate for them, although they were willing to submit to some trade regulations. They sent letters to the King, to the people of Great Britain, and to Canada. They also asked the people of Canada to join with them in the resistance.

This Congress also formed the *American Association,* for the non-importation and non-consumption of British goods. They also let it be understood that force used against Massachusetts would be met by force from the united colonies. Before adjourning, they called for another Congress to meet in May 1775.

THE SHOT HEARD AROUND THE WORLD

Massachusetts was declared to be in a state of rebellion. General Gage was ordered to subdue the insurrection. The order was also given to arrest Hancock, Samuel Adams and other patriot leaders. The patriot party was now obeying the Provincial Congress. They began to organize "minutemen" to assemble at a minute's warning and began to gather military stores.

General Gage sent soldiers from Boston to destroy some of these stores at Concord. Paul Revere on his famous ride, shouted the warning, "The regulars are coming!" The minutemen seized their rifles and came together at Lexington. When the British troops arrived they found less than 50 men. Major Pitcairn ordered them to disperse. When the minutemen refused, he ordered his soldiers to fire. Eight patriots fell and eight were wounded. The minutemen fell back, the soldiers went on and destroyed the ammunition at Concord, but at Concord Bridge they met 450 American resisters. The British turned to flee to Boston but from behind tree, house, haystack, and wall, deadly fire came their way. The British lost 273 men while the Americans lost 93. It had now been shown that American militiamen dared resist British regulars. The American Revolution had begun.

Patrick Henry at the Second Continental Congress expressed the feeling of many American patriots when he said, "We have petitioned, we have remonstrated, we have supplicated, we have prostrated ourselves at the foot of the throne, and it has been all in vain. We must fight! I repeat it sir, we must fight." Fight they did. Thus began what was to be a very difficult and desperate struggle.

THE DECLARATION OF INDEPENDENCE

To begin with the Americans were just fighting against oppression and to protect their rights. They still hoped to be reconciled with the mother country. After a year of fighting, they now wanted independence. Richard Lee of the Virginia delegation proposed his famous resolution: "that these United Colonies are, and of a right ought to be, free and independent states".

A committee was appointed to draw up the declaration. Thomas Jefferson wrote the declaration. Adams and Franklin suggested certain changes. On July 1^{st,} it was debated and on July 4, 1776, it was approved by the Second Continental Congress. The United States of America was born.

The Struggle had just begun. The war which had started for independence in 1775 would continue until the British finally surrendered on October 19, 1781. Before this, many bloody battles would be fought and the American Army would suffer a terrible hardship at Valley Forge. The physical struggle was intense, but just as intense was the spiritual struggle. So far Satan had failed miserably. America had broken free from bondage and had begun a new nation with a Constitution based primarily upon the Word of God. This outcome was not pleasing to Satan, but he was not about to give up. Both God and Satan had plans for America. In the next chapter we will see how this struggle develops.

CHAPTER 11

THE STRUGGLE FOR THE SOUL
OF AMERICA

Most of the colonists came to America for religious reasons. It is true that the first colonists to arrive in Virginia came for gold and riches but those who settled in New England later, came because of religious persecution in Europe.

The Declaration of Independence and later on the Constitution of the United States would be based upon the Bible. This was not to Satan's liking. Satan would later do everything in his power to use men to deny the biblical basis of America's founding.

The American War for Independence turned out completely different from the French Revolution, which would occur a few years later. France was ruled by a monarchy which was allied with the Catholic Church. They had severely put down the Protestant Reformation and were in control of most of the land and wealth of France. It would not be hard therefore for Satan to use the Illuminati to stir up strife, discontent and revolution. What started out in France as a quest for freedom soon turned into a reign of terror.

The American concept of freedom and liberty was based upon the Bible, and the tradition of freedom and liberty which had been worked out with the English Monarchy over the centuries. The French concept of freedom and liberty was an outgrowth of the Enlightenment and the age of reason. The French would fight for liberty because they were angry. The American colonists on the other hand fought for freedom and liberty because they firmly believed that they were so endowed by Almighty God.

Satan did not like this at all. In the future he would do all he possibly could to try to make Americans forget their Biblical heritage.

Before we continue to examine the struggle between God and Satan in America, we need to take a closer look at the French Revolution. In Chapter 10, we mentioned how the Illuminati had been exposed in Europe. After being exposed, Weishaupt ordered his followers to infiltrate Masonic Lodges. After becoming Masons they were to form their own secret society within these secret societies. There they would continue to work for the overthrow of all governments and put in its place a new world government. This new government would be ruled by the wise men of the Illuminati. Weishaupt's followers did just as they were ordered. They infiltrated the Masonic lodges in France and played the major role in bringing about the French Revolution.

Even though all the heads of church and state in Europe had been warned about the Illuminati conspiracy, they largely ignored the evidence and didn't take it seriously.

Among those who did not take the warnings seriously was the King of France, Louis XVI and his wife Marie Antoinette. Soon the slogans of liberty, equality, and fraternity would echo in France and the people would demand reform. One of the first things they did was to arrest the King in 1789. A few years later they executed the King. In 1793 the guillotine also severed the Queen's head.

The guillotine would soon become famous from June 1793 to July 1794 during the reign of terror in France. The mindless paranoia at that time resulted in 1,376 individuals being guillotined in only 47 days. Estimates of the death toll range between 15,000 and 40,000.

The great irony is that the French Revolution was all for nothing. Soon France would be ruled by Napoleon Bonaparte, and in 1814 King Louis XVIII would sit upon the throne of France. The Constitution, which the revolutionaries would draw up to secure liberty, equality, and fraternity, would soon be replaced with ten more constitutions. The United States, on the other hand, still has its first Constitution, although there are many today trying to overthrow it.

SATAN'S STRATEGY FOR AMERICA

Satan realized that if he were to accomplish his plans in America, he would have to use a different approach than he did in Europe. Most of the people who came to America did so in order to obtain religious freedom. They not only wanted freedom for themselves, but they were willing to extend that freedom to others. They exhibited a spirit of individualism and resourcefulness which was often lacking in those people who grew up in Europe.

The American Revolutionary War was already well in progress before influence of the Illuminati was able to reach America. Satan would now seek to influence the Masonic lodges in America just as he did in Europe. Many of America's leaders were already Masons, such as George Washington, Benjamin Franklin, and Thomas Jefferson. This did not give

Satan the advantage that one might suppose; because as soon as these men heard of the Illuminati and what was going on in Europe, they were in total opposition to it. Nevertheless, Satan persisted and was soon able to bring in his agents to seduce Masons and others in America to do his bidding.

MASONRY IN AMERICA

Masonry has been used by Satan as a tool to accomplish his primary purpose of breaking down the moral fiber of America and snatching the souls of men. Satan has used several different lures to hook men and bring them into Masonry.

1. **Greed:** I have been told that the way to get ahead in business is to become a Mason. Masons help one another. They don't testify against each other in court. You can even get out of speeding tickets.

2. **Deception:** Masonry claims that it is not a religion; that anyone who believes in God (whether he is a Christian, a Jew, a Hindu, or a Muslim) can become a member. Yet, they pray to the Great Architect of the Universe. When they reach the thirty-third degree they finally find out who their god really is. He is none other than Lucifer, the same god as the Illuminati.

3. **Charities:** There is no disputing the fact that Masons do many charitable deeds. For this they should be praised, but that doesn't wipe out all the negatives. For an extreme example, consider. Would you excuse a man for killing his wife because he was good to his mother?

THE STRUGGLE FOR THE SOUL OF AMERICA

There is very little that one could point to and say this is the way Masonry has harmed the social and moral fabric of America. Behind the scenes, however, Masonry has infiltrated churches, school boards, legislatures, and court rooms where they have adversely influenced society.

The most visible way that Masonry has influenced America is in the construction of its public buildings. Almost all government buildings have cornerstones laid and dedicated by Masons. The street layout of Washington, DC, was done by Masons. They incorporated their Masonic symbols in the layout of the streets, as is visible on the map.

At the nation's Capital Building we see the Compass and the Square. The White House forms the base of the Pentagram. In Masonry, the Pentagram is sometimes used alone and sometimes it is used with a goat's head superimposed inside of it. The goat's head is a symbol of Lucifer or Satan.

This does not mean that the government of the United States is satanic, but it certainly does mean Satan will use every way possible to influence it.

We will deal with Masonry and the Illuminati more latter. First though we need to consider some other strategies of Satan that would have a more immediate impact upon America

SLAVERY:

In Chapter 10 we mentioned that the first slaves arrived in America at Jamestown by a Dutch ship. It had been in battle with a Spanish ship and captured twenty African slaves. The Dutch ship was very much in need of repairs and food. The colonists were in need of able bodied labor. The colonists traded food for the slaves.

The citizens of Jamestown decided to treat the first Africans in America as indentured servants which meant that after a stated period, they would be freed.

The transformation from indentured servitude to racial slavery happened gradually. There are no laws regarding slavery early in Virginia's history, but that soon changed.

During the British colonial period, every colony had slaves. Those in the North were primarily house servants. In the South, slaves were mostly used by rich farmers and plantation owners. Backwoods farmers seldom owned slaves.

Many people realized the terrible evil of slavery, but they were caught in a trap. They didn't know how to get out. Both George Washington and Thomas Jefferson owned slaves but came to regret it. George Washington did not seem troubled about owning slaves in his early years, but later he wanted to be done with slavery. He thought about selling some of the younger slaves, but many of their parents and grandparents were old and in need of care. Washington was obliged to provide for them and he didn't want to break up families.

When he died, he stipulated in his will that all the slaves were to be freed.

Thomas Jefferson recognized the terrible evil of slavery, and desired to set his slaves free as soon as he could get out of debt. Unfortunately, he was never able to get out of debt and died broke. Jefferson finally emancipated his five most trusted slaves; the others were sold after his death to pay his debts.

Jefferson, in writing about slavery said, "We have the wolf by the ears; and we can neither hold him, nor safely let him go. Justice is in one scale, and self-preservation in the other."

Jefferson attempted many times to abolish or limit slavery. He believed that it was the responsibility of the state and society to free all slaves. In 1769, as a member of the House of Burgesses, he proposed the emancipation of all the slaves in Virginia, but was voted down.

In his first draft of the Declaration of Independence, Jefferson condemned the British crown for sponsoring the importation of slavery to the colonies, charging that the crown "has waged cruel war against human nature itself, violating its most sacred rights of life and liberty in the persons of a distant people who never offended him, captivating and carrying them into slavery in another hemisphere". This language was dropped from the Declaration at the request of delegates from South Carolina and Georgia.

In some cases slaves were treated horribly, but in other cases they were almost like a part of the slave owners' family. In either case, the institution of slavery was a terrible evil.

As we look at it today we might ask, "How could a nation that believed in the God of the Bible do such things?" You have to remember the times in which they lived. Slavery was practiced in Africa and all Muslim countries of the Middle East. Europeans did not practice slavery, but they had indentured servants who for their time of servitude were slaves. Europe also had its castles where serfs toiled. They were little better off than slaves. If you think society is better today, consider this question. "How could a nation like the United States, where most people claim to be Christian, murder over a million babies in the womb each year?"

Satan knew that he had a good thing going. What could be more delightful than to see the contradiction in "all men are created equal" and then deny to others their God given rights? Satan knew full well that one day America would pay a terrible price.

Just as demand for slaves was increasing, in 1808 Congress banned any further imports of slaves. Therefore any new slaves would have to be born from the slaves already here.

Opposition to slavery continued to grow, especially in the Northern States. Slavery was very profitable on the large plantations in the South, but it was not very profitable for industrial applications in the North. Soon the whole nation was split between the free states of the North and the slave states of the South. As new states were added in the West, there was a struggle as to whether they were to be a free states or slave states.

When Abraham Lincoln was elected in 1860, he was elected without being on the ballot of ten southern states. Seven of those southern states declared their secession from the union even before Lincoln took office. Many slave owners in the South feared that the Republicans would abolish slavery in states where it already existed, and that if four million slaves were suddenly freed, it would bring about disaster to the slave owners and for the economy.

They also argued that banning slavery in new states would upset what they saw as a delicate balance of Free States and Slave States. They feared domination by the industrial North because of its preference for high tariffs on imported goods.

It wasn't long before hostilities broke out on April 12, 1861, when Confederate forces attacked Fort Sumter in South Carolina. Thus began the deadliest war in American history. Soldiers killed were about 620,000 plus an undetermined number of civilian casualties. The war brought with it terrible hardship and suffering especially for people in the South. General Sherman of the Union Army, toward the end of the war, captured and burnt Atlanta. Then he began his famous march to the sea in which he devastated a hundred-mile-wide swath of Georgia. Confederate resistance collapsed after Lee surrendered to Grant in April 1865.

Slavery in the United States finally came to an end and the Union was restored, but at what a horrible price. Satan had done his work well. Satan used greed, envy, fear, hypocrisy, and rivalry to nearly bring the United States to an end. Satan had won only a partial victory, but he would certainly continue to promote racial tension and discord. For the time being, however, we need to look at some other areas of Satan's schemes.

CENTRAL BANKING

Through long experience Satan knew that money and power go together. Now he would try to bring the banking system that he had developed to America.

During the Colonial Period, the American colonies were doing quite well without a banking system. When the officials of the Bank of England asked Franklin how he could account for the new-found prosperity of the colonies, he replied:

> "That is simple. In the colonies we issue our own money. It is called Colonial Scrip. We issue it in proper proportion to the demands of trade and industry to make the products pass easily from the producers to the consumers...In this manner, creating for ourselves our own paper money, we control its purchasing power, and we have interest to pay to no one."

This was just common sense to Franklin, but you can imagine the impact it had at the Bank of England. America had learned the secret of money, and that just would not do. As a result, Parliament hurriedly passed the Currency Act of 1764. This prohibited colonial officials from issuing their own money and ordered them to pay all future taxes in gold or silver coins. This had two immediate effects. First of all, what little gold and silver were in the colonies began to flow back to England. The second effect was to plunge the colonies into a depression, because they lacked the necessary medium of exchange to carry on business.

Writing in his autobiography, Franklin said: ***"In one year, the conditions were so reversed that the era of prosperity ended, and a depression set in, to such an extent that the streets of the Colonies were filled with unemployed."***

Franklin claims that this was the basic cause for the American Revolution. As Franklin put it in his autobiography:

"The Colonies would gladly have borne the little tax on tea and other matters had it not been that England took away from the Colonies their money, which created unemployment and dissatisfaction."

In 1774, Parliament passed the Stamp Act which required that a stamp be placed on every instrument of commerce, indicating payment of tax in gold. Less than two weeks later, the Massachusetts Committee of Safety passed a resolution directing the issuance of more colonial currency and honoring the currency of other colonies.

By the time the first shots were fired in Massachusetts at Concord and Lexington, the colonies had been drained of their gold and silver by British taxation. As a result, the Continental government had no choice but to print its own paper money to finance the war.

On June 10 and June 22, 1775, the "Congress of the Colonies" resolved to issue paper money based on the credit and faith of the "United Colonies". At the start of the Revolution, the U.S. (colonial) money supply stood at $12 million. By the end of the war, it was nearly $500 million. This was partly a result of massive British counterfeiting. As a result, the currency was virtually worthless. Shoes sold for $5,000 a pair.

Colonial scrip had worked fine before the war, because just enough was issued to enable trade and counterfeiting was minimal. It had worked so well that the Bank of England had Parliament outlaw it. During the war, the British deliberately sought to undermine it by counterfeiting it in England and shipping it to the colonies.

Because so much money was printed, colonial money quickly became worthless. That is where the expression *"Not worth a continental."* comes from. This helped open the door for Satan to gain control of the money system.

Satanic control of the money system in the United States came about gradually. By 1781, the US was in a crisis and the treasury was in debt by $25 million. The war with England was still in progress, and public credit had collapsed. The Continental Congress then appointed Robert Morris to become Finance Minister. Three days after his appointment, Morris proposed the establishment of a national bank.

The Continental Congress then proceeded to charter the Bank of North America which opened in 1782. The purpose of the Bank was to try and bring about a degree of financial stability. The Bank was funded partly by a loan which Morris had obtained from the Netherlands and France. He then issued new paper currency backed by this supply. He also managed to meet the interest rates on the debt which he estimated to be about thirty million dollars, but the value of American currency however, continued to plummet. Therefore in 1785, the Bank's charter was not renewed.

It was probably not known at the time but Morris received much of his ideas for a national bank from Alexander Hamilton, who was still serving in the military. In fact, the year before the Bank of North America was established, Hamilton had written Morris a letter, saying, *"A national debt, if it is not excessive, will be to us a national blessing,"*

During the Revolutionary War, Hamilton served as an artillery captain and was an aid to General George Washington.

Later he served as the first Secretary of the Treasury. Hamilton believed in the importance of a strong central government. He admired the success of the British system, especially its strong financial and trade networks along with its strong central bank.

This admiration of the Bank of England and a strong central bank was not shared by Thomas Jefferson and James Madison. They had seen the problems caused by the Bank of England. As Jefferson later put it:

> "If the American people ever allow private banks to control the issue of their currency, first by inflation, then by deflation, the banks and the corporations which grow up around them will deprive the people of all property until their children wake up homeless on the continent their fathers conquered."

Unfortunately, Alexander Hamilton was a tool of the international bankers. Now as the newly-appointed first Secretary of the Treasury in 1790, he proposed a bill to Congress calling for a new privately-owned central bank. It was that very same year that Meyer Rothschild made his pronouncement from his flagship bank in Frankfort:

> "Let me issue and control a nation's money and I care not who writes its laws."

After a year of intense debate, in 1791, Congress passed Hamilton's bank bill and gave it a 20-year charter. The new bank was to be called the First Bank of the United States.

Both Madison and Jefferson strongly opposed the bank bill, but eventually Hamilton convinced Washington to sign the bill. To convince Washington, he developed the idea of **"implied powers"** in the Constitution.

Jefferson correctly predicted the dire consequences of opening such a **Pandora's Box** which would allow judges to "imply" whatever they wished.

The Bank had been promoted to Congress as a way to bring stability to the banking system and to eliminate inflation. So what happened? Over the first five years, the U.S. government borrowed $8.2 million from the Bank of the United States. In that period, prices rose by 72%.

Jefferson as the new Secretary of State, watched with sorrow as the United States borrowed money and became obligated to the banks, but there was nothing he could do to stop it.

> "I wish it were possible to obtain a single amendment to
> our Constitution - taking from the federal government
> the power of borrowing."

In 1811, a bill was put before Congress to renew the charter of the Bank of the United States. Both Pennsylvania and Virginia passed resolutions asking Congress to kill the Bank. The newspapers called the Bank a great swindle, a vulture, and a poisonous snake.

James Madison was now President. He had long opposed the Bank. When it came up for a vote his Vice President, George Clinton, broke the tie in the Senate. The First Bank of the United States was no more.

Nathan Rothschild is said to have warned that the United States would find itself involved in a most disastrous war if the Bank's charter was not renewed. Within five months, England attacked and the United States was drawn into the War of 1812. The war didn't last very long because the British were still fighting Napoleon. The war ended in a draw in 1814.

While the Bankers were temporarily defeated, they certainly did not give up. It only took them another two years to get the federal government to charter the Second Bank of the United States (1816-1836). It was basically a copy of the First Bank.

The Second Bank of the United States was backed by the Rothschilds who very much wanted to increase their control in the United States.

After Napoleon's defeat on June 18, 1815, as we saw in Chapter 9, the Rothschilds practically owned Great Britain and had taken control of the Bank of England. Now with Napoleon's defeat they also began to dominate the Bank of France.

It didn't take very long before the American people had once again had just about enough of monetary manipulations on the part of the Second Bank of the U.S. Opponents of the Bank nominated Andrew Jackson, the hero of the Battle of New Orleans, to run for president. The Bank had long-ago learned how the political process could be controlled with money, but to their surprise in 1828, Jackson was swept into office. Jackson was determined to kill the Bank at the first opportunity, and wasted no time to trying to do so.

Since the Bank didn't come up for renewal until 1836 Jackson contented himself with rooting out the Bank's sympathizers from government service. He fired 2,000 of the 11,000 employees of the federal government.

In 1832 the Bank thought that it would strike a blow against Jackson since he was coming up for re-election by asking

Congress to renew its charter early but they underestimated Jackson. He vetoed the bill. In his veto message he noted that much of the bank stock was owned by foreigners who have no loyalty to our country.

He said, ***"Controlling our currency, receiving our public moneys, and holding thousands of our citizens in dependence...would be more formidable and dangerous than a military power of the enemy"*** He added, ***"It is to be regretted that the rich and powerful too often bend the acts of government to their selfish purposes"***

Congress was unable to override Jackson's veto. Now Jackson had to stand for re-election. Jackson took his argument directly to the people.

The Bank had Senator Henry Clay run against Jackson and funded his campaign with over $3,000,000 which was an enormous sum at that time, Jackson was still re-elected by a landslide.

Despite his presidential victory, Jackson knew the battle was only beginning. Jackson ordered his Secretary of the Treasury to start removing the government's deposits from the Second Bank of the U.S. and to start placing them in state banks. After the first two Secretaries of the Treasury refused to comply, he then appointed Roger B. Taney who did as he was told and withdrew government funds from the bank, starting on October 1, 1833. Jackson thought he had won, but the Bank was not through fighting.

Its head, Nlcholas Biddle, used his influence to get the Senate to reject Taney's nomination. Then, Biddle threatened the U.S. with an economic depression if the Bank was not re-chartered.

He made the statement. ***"This worthy President thinks that because he has scalped Indians and imprisoned Judges, he is to have his way with the Bank. He is mistaken."***
Next he admitted that the bank was going to make money scarce in order to force Congress to restore the Bank:

> "Nothing but widespread suffering will produce any effect on Congress...Our only safety is in pursuing a steady course of firm restriction and I have no doubt that such a course will ultimately lead to restoration of the currency and the re-charter of the Bank."

Biddle intended to use the money contraction power given to the Bank to cause a massive depression until America gave in.

Nicholas Biddle made good on his threat. The Bank sharply contracted the money supply by calling in old loans and refusing to extend new ones. A financial panic ensued, followed by a deep economic depression. Of course, Biddle blamed Jackson for the crash.

His plan was working very well. Wages and prices sagged. Unemployment soared along with business bankruptcies.

The nation quickly went into an uproar. Newspaper editors blasted Jackson in editorials. Within a few months, Congress assembled in what was called the "Panic Session."

Six months after he had withdrawn funds from the bank, Jackson was officially censured by a resolution which passed the Senate by a vote of 26 to 20.

If Congress could override Jackson's veto, the Bank would be granted a monopoly over America's money, for another 20 years or more. This would give it enough time to consolidate its power.

Just when it looked like Jackson and the American people would lose, the Governor of Pennsylvania, where the 2nd Bank was headquartered, came out supporting the President and strongly criticized the Bank. On top of that, word got out about how Biddle had bragged about the Bank's plan to crash the economy.

In April of 1834, the House of Representatives voted 134 to 82 against re-chartering the Bank and they then voted to investigate whether the Bank had caused the crash. Biddle refused to cooperate, but he was later arrested and charged with fraud.

On January 8, 1835, eleven years after taking office, Jackson paid off the final installment on the national debt. This debt had occurred because the government had allowed the banks to issue currency to buy government bonds. The government could have simply issued Treasury notes without such debt. He was the only President ever to pay off the national debt.

A few weeks later, on January 30, 1835, an assassin by the name of Richard Lawrence tried to shoot President Jackson. Both pistols misfired. Lawrence was later found not guilty by reason of insanity. After his release, he bragged to friends that powerful people in Europe had put him up to the task and promised to protect him if he were caught.

The following year, when its charter ran out, the Second Bank of the United States ceased functioning as the nation's central bank.

What followed from 1837-1862, is known as the Free Banking Era. During this time only State Chartered Banks existed. They could issue bank notes against gold and silver and the various States regulated their reserve requirements, interest rates etc.

Many of the banks were unstable however, and about half of the banks failed. They also continued one of the most undesirable features of a bank which is fractional reserve banking. In fractional reserve banking a bank will take $1,000 in deposits and then lend out up to $10,000 which it creates out of nothing through a bookkeeping entry. You can be sure though that it charges interest on every bit of it. Everything works fine for the bank as long as people have faith in the bank. If however, they lose faith in the bank and want their deposits back the bank will then be in trouble because for every $1,000 that people want back, the bank will have to call in $10,000 worth of loans which will simply be impossible.

BANKING AND THE CIVIL WAR

The freeing of the slaves, as laudable as that goal might have been, was not the main reason for the Civil War; it was instead the result of the war. The Northern States had far more industry than the Southern States and they used Congress to pass tariffs on manufactured items in order to keep Southern states from buying cheaper European goods. Europe retaliated by stopping cotton imports from the South. The result was that the Southern States were forced to pay more for their necessities of life while their income from cotton exports went down. The North was out for money. The South was trying to protect its way of life and Lincoln was trying to protect the union. One of the most overlooked factors in the Civil War was the role that the Central Bankers played.

Since the defeat of the Second Bank of the United States in 1836 the central bankers in the United States were more or less in hibernation just waiting for the right time to come out of their cave. In the mean time America had been flourishing without them. As far as the bankers were concerned, that was a bad example to the rest of the world. Finally, they saw their opportunity to exploit the tensions between the North and the South. If they couldn't get their central bank any other way they would use war, blood, and debt to achieve their ends.

One month after the inauguration of Abraham Lincoln, the first shots of the American Civil War were fired at Fort Sumter, South Carolina on April 12, 1861.

In 1876, Otto von Bismarck, Chancellor of Germany is quoted as saying:

> "It is not to be doubted, I know of absolute certainty," Bismarck declared, "that the division of the United States into two federations of equal power was decided long before the Civil War by the high financial powers of Europe. These bankers were afraid that the United States, if they remained as one block and were to develop as one nation, would attain economic and financial independence, which would upset the capitalist domination of Europe over the world."

A few months after the war began, central bankers loaned Napoleon III of France 210 million francs to seize Mexico and station troops along the southern border of the U.S. They wanted to violate the Monroe Doctrine and return Mexico, Central, and South America to colonial rule.

At the same time, Great Britain moved 11,000 troops into Canada and positioned them along America's northern border. Lincoln was well aware that there was more at stake than just the differences between the North and the South. That's why his emphasis was always on the *"Union"*.

To fight a war though, Lincoln needed money. He tried to borrow from the banks, but they wanted to charge outrageous interest, between 24 – 36%. Lincoln said thanks, but no thanks.

Lincoln sent for his old friend Colonel Dick Taylor and asked him how to finance the war. Taylor replied:

> "Why, Lincoln, that is easy; just get Congress to pass a bill authorizing the printing of full legal tender treasury notes... pay your soldiers with them and go ahead and win your war with them also."

That's exactly what Lincoln did and from 1862 to 1865 he printed up $432,000,000 of the new bills which had green ink on the back side which distinguished them from private bank notes. That's why they were called *"Greenbacks."*

No interest of course had to be paid out to anyone for this new money. Money created by the government instead of the banks would save the taxpayers immense sums of interest.

To be sure, what Lincoln had done did not go unnoticed by the central bankers who already had control of the banks and newspaper in Great Britain. This editorial appeared in the London Times.

> "If this mischievous financial policy, which has its origin in North America, shall become indurate down to a fixture, then the Government will furnish its own money without cost. It will pay off debts and be without debt. It will have all the money necessary to carry on its commerce. It will become prosperous without precedent in the history of the world. The brains and wealth of all countries will go to North America. That country must be destroyed or it will destroy every monarchy on the globe."

The central bankers concern was that if this American experiment were allowed to stand they would lose control over the Kings of Europe.

In America the bankers were just as alarmed. Within four days after the passage of the law that allowed Greenbacks to be printed the bankers met in Washington to discuss the situation and to figure out a way to undermine the value of the Greenbacks. They insisted that greenbacks not be used to pay import duties or interest on the public debt and banks were used to slap a surcharge on Greenbacks. This undermined the confidence people had in Greenbacks. Their scheme was so effective that in 1863 Lincoln finally gave into the pressure from the banks and Congress which produced the *"National Banking Act."* This act gave the National Banks the exclusive power to create money. From this point on U.S. Money would be created as a debt with the interest to be paid to the bankers.

The Civil War finally came to an end. Had Lincoln been permitted to live he would have surely killed the National Banks monopoly on money which the bankers had coerced out of him during the war.

On April 14, 1865, just five days after Lee surrendered to Grant, Lincoln was shot by John Wilkes Booth, at Ford's theater.

In 1934, Gerald G. McGeer, a Canadian attorney made a stunning charge before the House of Commons in which he blasted Canada's debt-based money system.

McGeer had obtained evidence which had been deleted from the public record of the trial of John Wilkes Booth, after Booth's death. It had been provided to him by Secret Service agents. McGeer said it showed that Booth was a mercenary working for the international bankers. According to an article in the Vancouver Sun of May 2, 1934:

"Abraham Lincoln was assassinated through the machinations of a group representative of the international bankers, who feared the United States President's national credit ambitions...There was only one group in the world at that time who had any reason to desire the death of Lincoln...They were the men opposed to his national currency programme and who had fought him throughout the whole Civil War on his policy of Greenback currency."

Sadly, this wasn't the last time an American President would be assassinated. In 1881, James A. Garfield was elected President. Garfield understood how the economy was being manipulated by the bankers. He had been chairman of the Appropriations Committee, and was a member of the Banking and Currency Committee while in Congress. After his inauguration, he slammed the Money Changers.

"Whoever controls the volume of money in any country is absolute master of all industry and commerce...and when you realize that the entire system is very easily controlled, one way or another, by a few powerful men at the top, you will not have to be told how periods of inflation and depression originate."

Garfield understood. Within a few weeks of making this statement, on July 2 of 1881, President Garfield was assassinated.

As we noted earlier in this chapter there was an attempted assassination of President Jackson after he had killed the Second Bank of the United States and there would be another successful assassination in the Twentieth Century after President Kennedy had some treasury money printed.

There were two things the Central Bankers wanted. First they wanted a privately owned central bank under their complete control and secondly they wanted an American currency issued by them and backed by their gold.

The bankers still didn't have the central bank that they wanted but they would seek to get rid of the greenbacks, contract the money supply by calling in loans and not issuing new ones, and they would demonetize silver. They would continue to cause depressions and scarcity until they got what they wanted. Finally in 1913, they got what they wanted but we will deal with that in a later chapter. First we need to go back a few years to deal with some other facets of the Satanic Conspiracy during the 19th Century.

THE POPULATION TIME BOMB:

In 1798, Thomas Robert Malthus published a pamphlet on the principle of population. He said that population increases geometrically, while the means of subsistence increases arithmetically. Therefore, the population will exceed the means to sustain life. If food supply is increased, the population will increase even more until the population will have to be thinned out through war, disease, pestilence, or famine. He said this process has been at work all through the centuries and will continue until the end of time. Needless to say, these theories have influenced opinion concerning eugenics, population control, and abortion.

Without a doubt, there is merit to Thomas Malthus' theories. The question we must consider though is; do we deal with population control by our own methods and reasoning or let God be God? And let him deal with it.

Unfortunately, mankind has always tried to deal with things according to their own strength and reasoning. Man's abilities are limited, while God's ability is unlimited. God is well able to control population growth without the need for war, disease, famine, or abortion. If man however, wants to see God take control, he will have to put his trust in God, and wait patiently to see what God will do. This however is something that mankind has not been inclined to do.

COMMUNISM:

Karl Marx has been credited as the father of communism since he and Friedrich Engels published "The Communist Manifesto" on February 21, 1848. Karl was the third of seven children of a Jewish family in Prussia. His father was descended from a long line of rabbis but converted to Christianity when the Prussian authorities would not allow him to continue to practice law as a Jew.

Marx was influenced in his thinking by "Young Hegelians" who were prominent in Berlin at the time. They had accepted part of the teaching of the German philosopher Georg W. F. Hegel but had rejected the God part. They made use of Hegel's dialectical method, separated from its theological content, as a powerful weapon for the critique of established religion and politics.

In 1843, Marx met Friedrich Engels. Engels came to Paris where Marx was now living to show him his book, "The Condition of the Working Class in England in 1844."

In 1845, Marx was banished from Paris as a dangerous revolutionary. He then went to Brussels, Belgium where he and Engels joined a German secret society called the "Communist League." At the league's request they authored the "Communist Manifesto" in 1848.

The Communist League was founded as the "League of the - Just" by German workers in 1836. This was to begin with a Christian Communist group. Their motto was "All men are Brothers" and its goals were "the establishment of the Kingdom of God on Earth, based on the ideals of love of one's neighbor, equality and justice".

The Communist League was created in London in June 1847 out of a merger of the League of the Just and of the fifteen-man Communist Correspondence Committee, headed by Karl Marx and the League was stripped of its Christian character.

In 1867, Marx published, "Das Kapital" which is a critical analysis of capitalism and its practical economic applications. In this book he also lays out his rational for Communism.

THE THEORY OF EVOLUTION:

In 1859, Charles Darwin published a book called the "Origin of the Species." The theory of evolution contained in this book altered the way people thought about God, religion, education and science to this very day. While the theory of evolution is unproved and un-provable, it appears to be the official religion of the educational community.

Of all the various philosophies that we have talked about evolution is without a doubt the most destructive. It has been a major stumbling block for many Christians who have struggled between believing in God who created all things or believing the pseudo-science of the evolutionary theory. That alone makes evolution the most destructive philosophy in history, but there is more.

What many people do not realize is that evolution has also been responsible for the death of many millions of people on this earth. In 1867 Karl Marx, in his book "Das Kapital" based his theories of communism on evolution. Later on for the purposes of establishing communism in Russia, 35 million peasants were forced to starve to death. When communism came to China, a similar thing happened with millions of Chinese being put to death.

Evolution was also at the root of Margaret Sanger's Eugenics. This became the basis for Adolf Hitler's attempt to build a master race by exterminating the Jews. It is also the basis for the abortion industry today, which has already killed over 40 million babies in the United States.

REVIEW OF THE SPIRITUAL BATTLES OF THE 19TH CENTURY:

By the end of the 19th century, Satan was well advanced in his plans to set up the final conspiracy. Some of Satan's accomplishments were as follows:

1. Satan instigated slavery to bring a curse upon the United States, which almost destroyed the nation.
2. Satan was able to get his people in the banking system to gain control over the money system. He would use that money to reward those who would do his bidding.
3. In Europe, Satan used the philosophies of rationalism and nihilism along with the theory

of evolution, and communism to change the course of future history.

4. Satan was able to bring humanistic philosophies into the Theological Seminaries. This would very quickly have a devastating effect on the Churches in Europe and have a similar effect on many of the Churches in the United States during the 20th Century.

I am sure Satan must have been very proud of all his accomplishments but he knew full well that in many ways he had failed.

In spite of all that he had been able to accomplish England was sending missionaries all over the world. Revivals were taking place in America. When the Lutheran Church became corrupt in Germany a group came to America to establish a more Bible believing church. Satan didn't consider it a defeat however, but just another step in his effort to defeat God's plan and purpose. Satan already had great plans for the Twentieth Century.

CHAPTER 12

THE TWENTIETH CENTURY (1900-1940)

N ow in the twentieth century Satan would try to implement his scheme to bring the whole world under his control. He would try to banish faith and the true worship of God while seeking all worship and adoration for himself. While his plans involved the whole world he would particularly target the United States because of its influence and power over other countries.

First, he planned get the money and banking system under his control in order to supply the money needed to carry out his other plans. Second, he would try to destroy Christian belief and morals. In order to accomplish this he would use Religious and Educational Institutions, Wars, Financial Distress, and the Media to accomplish his purposes. Without question Satan has to a large degree succeeded in his goals. In the rest of this Chapter we will take a close look at Satan's war against God during the twentieth century.

Satan had great plans for the twentieth century. He would use the tactics and philosophies which had worked so well in Europe to destroy faith and morals in the United States. He would continue to pursue war as a means to decimate mankind, promote wickedness and brutality. He would get his people into educational institutions in order to corrupt the youth and get them to think his way. First though he needed money. Money it has been said is the answer to all things. How was Satan to get the money? He would get it through the banking system.

Finally, in 1913 Satan got his way. Satan had his people call a secret meeting of rich and powerful bankers to Jekyll Island, which is an island off of the southeast coast of Georgia, where they plotted the takeover of the United States money system.

They would accomplish their purpose, the tried and true way. They would help politicians get elected through campaign contributions and persuasion. When a man of great wealth and influence approaches a political hopeful and says, *I think you have promise, I think you might make a great Senator. Why don't we get together and talk about it? I have $100,000 that I would like to contribute to a worthy cause.* What do you think that politician is likely to do? Of course he is going to talk to this wealthy and powerful man. After the politician has been thoroughly wined, dined and influenced he no doubt would deny even to himself that he had been bought and paid for but he was.

Prior to 1913, America was a prosperous, powerful, and growing nation, at peace with its neighbors and the envy of the world. But in December 23, 1913, everything changed. The conspirators waited in Washington until most of those who opposed the legislation went home for the Christmas holidays. They then assembled Congress and passed the Glass-Owen bill, which soon became known as The Federal Reserve Act. President Wilson immediately signed it.

If you would like to get the full story of how this came about, read "The Creature from Jekyll Island," by G. Edward

Griffin. This legislation authorized the establishment of the Federal Reserve Corporation, which had authority to create money out of nothing and lend it to the member banks and the United States Government with interest.

President Woodrow Wilson eventually came to realize that he had been deceived into signing the Federal Reserve Act. But now it was too late. The following is a quote from President Wilson.

> "A great industrial Nation is controlled by its system of credit. Our system of credit is concentrated. The growth of the Nation and all our activities are in the hands of a few men. We have come to be one of the worst ruled, one of the most completely controlled and dominated Governments in the world - no longer a Government of free opinion no longer a Government by conviction and vote of the majority, but a Government by the opinion and duress of small groups of dominant men".

*(Just before he died, Wilson is reported to have stated to friends that he had been **"deceived"** and that **"I have betrayed my Country".** He was referring to the Federal Reserve Act which he had signed into law.)*

THE FEDERAL RESERVE SYSTEM:

In a popular TV Series **"Drag Net"** some years ago, Sergeant Friday often said to a witnesses, *"Just the FACTS PLEASE."* That's what we need to know about the Federal Reserve. There is often a great deal of difference between the myths believed by most people regarding the Federal Reserve and what the actual facts are.

MYTH: The Federal Reserve is owned and controlled by the U. S. Government.

FACT: The Federal Reserve is a private Bank owned by a cartel of Bankers. Many of the original stockholders were not even American citizens. Nor is the Federal Reserve controlled by the Government. When congress wanted to audit the Federal Reserve, the Bank told them to get lost. The Federal Reserve is Federal in name only. They are just as much Federal as the Boy Scouts. They were both chartered by Congress.

MYTH: The name Federal Reserve would seem to indicate that they have a monetary reserve.

FACT: False. The Federal Reserve has no reserves. They create the money they need out of nothing. They simply have it printed or push a few buttons on a computer.

MYTH: The Federal Reserve would bring about financial stability.

FACT: Nothing could be further from the truth. The banks created a series of panics in the last quarter of the 19th Century and a particularly sever panic in 1907 in order to get the people to support a National Bank which was supposed to end financial panics. Instead of ending panics the Federal Reserve brought the country into the worst depression in history. Just 16 years later the stock market crashed and the United States entered the Great Depression.

Just 15 years after the crash of the stock market 730 delegates from 44 nations gathered in Bretton Woods, New Hampshire during the first three weeks of July 1944 in order to try to fix the world financial problems partly brought upon the world by the Federal Reserve. At this time they established the International Monetary Fund. (IMF).

In 1971 things had gone from bad to worse. The United States had been trying to maintain the value of the dollar by selling gold to foreign countries for $35 an ounce. In the meantime the US had been increasing the money supply which devalues the dollar. Some countries, France in particular, realized the dollar was being cheapened and began to exchange dollars for gold. President Nixon realized that it wouldn't take long for all the gold to be shipped overseas if he were to continue to sell gold at $35 an ounce. He therefore closed the gold window. He told the world that the United States would no longer sell gold for $35 an ounce and that gold would now be sold on the open market for whatever price it would bring.

In less than 60 years the Federal Reserve had brought the United States to bankruptcy twice. The U.S. in effect declared bankruptcy on the American people in 1933 when it confiscated all the gold and then doubled the price on the gold which it used for international settlements. Then in 1971 Nixon declared the U.S. bankrupt to the world when he refused to exchange dollars for gold.

Now the United States has again come to the point of bankruptcy only this time it will not be so easy to recover from it.

WHAT MAKES THE FEDERAL RESERVE SO BAD, AND IF IT'S THAT BAD WHY DON'T WE GET RID OF IT?

The Federal Reserve is by nature financially unstable because of the way it is designed. All the money that the Federal Reserve loans is money that it creates out of thin air and loans into existence. The money loaned is sufficient to pay back the loan but the interest must be paid back from other funds.

In this way it is not long before the money which is loaned into existence replaces all the original money. Soon no one has any money except that which has been borrowed. In order to keep commerce going, the banks have to keep loaning more and more money. As the money supply increases it buys less and less. That is why 2 cents in 1900 would buy as much as a dollar does today. That is also why very few people actually own the house in which they live. If you owe money on it, you don't own it. If you don't believe me try missing a few payments and see who owns it.

While the Federal Reserve has not been good for the people of the United States or the world, it has most certainly fulfilled the purposes for which it was designed. America now had a central bank just like all the European Countries and the people pulling the strings of power in Europe would join with those pulling the strings of power in America to try to accomplish Satan's goal of uniting the whole world under his dominion.

WHAT IS THE REAL PURPOSE OF THE FEDERAL RESERVE?

The real purpose of the Federal Reserve was to provide money and power to those men who because of their greed and ambition Satan could use to take over not only the banks; but the government, educational institutions, influence the churches, provoke war and bloodshed, and try to thwart God's purposes for America.

There is a group of men who are so rich and powerful that they are able to pull the strings in such a way that Kings, Rulers, Presidents, Parliaments, and Congresses do its bidding. They are referred to as the "Elite" or "the powers that be." No names are ever given because these men remain hidden.

They don't want any publicity. If they are able to be identified they might also be killed. Do they know that they are actively serving Satan? Some of them may not believe in God or Satan but most of them probably realize that they are in the service of Satan. One of their organizations, Free Masonry leaves open the question of who the "Great Architect of the Universe" is until the 33rd degree when it is revealed that the god they serve is Lucifer or Satan. While it may be difficult or impossible to identify a lot of the top generals in Satan's army it is not too hard to spot his underlings.

Once the Bankers and the moneyed elite had the Federal Reserve in place they lost no time using it to their full advantage. Naturally the first thing they wanted to do was to get the United States to borrow money from them so that they could collect interest. That would happen very soon.

WORLD WAR I

World War I began June 28, 1914 when Archduke Franz Ferdinand of Austria heir to the Austro-Hungarian throne and his wife Sophie were assassinated by Gavrilo Princip a Bosnian-Serb. He and other Serbs were seeking independence from Austria–Hungry. There were peacemaking attempts but within weeks almost all of Europe was at war and before it was over even the United States was involved. It quickly became one of deadliest conflicts in history, with over 15 million people killed. It was said to be the **War to End All Wars,** but it was just the beginning of even greater conflicts.

On November 7, 1916, Woodrow Wilson was elected for his second term as President of the United States with this campaign slogan: "He kept us out of the war", but in April 1917 the United States entered the war.

By the time the war was over in 1919 the whole face of Europe had been changed with many new smaller states. The German Empire had been overthrown and Austro-Hungarian, the Russian, and Ottoman Empires had collapsed and broken up. The ancient monarchies were replaced by democratic, socialist, or communist republics.

In January 1918 President Woodrow Wilson made public his 14 points as the path to permanent world peace. November 11 of that year the war ends. At eleven o'clock on the eleventh day of the eleventh month of 1918, Germany and the Allies sign an Armistice.

Even though the Germans surrendered based on Wilson's 14 points when it came time to draw up the peace treaty, France and England ignored the 14 points. Instead, they sought vengeance against the Germans. They insisted on war reparations which caused hyper inflation in the new German republic and soon caused it to fail. This government was then replaced by Adolph Hitler and Nazi Germany was born. Because of the Allied greed and vengeance they had now sown the seeds of World War II.

Even though Woodrow Wilson had worked hard to set up the League of Nations, (which was supposed to prevent war ever occurring again) it was rejected by Congress and the United States never became a part of the League of Nations.

The League of Nations organized at the end of World War I was a political debating society for the nations of the world which the United States never joined. When a crisis would arise the League would talk about it and pass resolutions but was completely powerless to affect any change in the outcome. While the League of Nations accomplished nothing good no doubt Satan was well pleased because it succeeded it getting many people to start thinking about a New World Order.

THE CAUSES AND RESULTS OF WWI

The History books list the jealousies, greed, and ambitions of various rulers. The real reasons though are somewhat different. Satan wanted to foment instability and bring down kingdoms in order to replace them with a government that would better serve him. For this purpose he used his servants, THE POWERS THAT BE, and the bankers to use fear and greed to stir up the people and their rulers.

The bankers went along with Satan's plan because they knew that the way for them to increase their riches and power was to lend money to governments to fight wars. The rulers cooperated because they wanted to increase their land and power. The people went along because Satan convinced both sides that it would be an easy, painless, victory. Of course it was all a lie. The War was not quick, easy, or painless.

Germany had been so weakened through war, defeat, and now the reparations which led to hyper-inflation that it was now easy for Satan to put his man Adolph Hitler in power. With Satan's help Hitler would soon restore Germany's economic, military, and manufacturing power in order to establish the Third Reich. The Third Reich was to be a re-incarnation of the Roman Empire which would conquer the world and last for a thousand years. Hitler was smart, ruthless and would do Satan's bidding to try to destroy the Jews. Satan detested the Jews because they were a people that God has so favored. God had made many promises to the Jews and as long as they existed they would remind people of Jesus. Satan could never fully discredit Jesus as long as the Jews were around because they were a constant, silent testimony of the fact that God is faithful to His Word.

Great Britain had been greatly weakened economically by the war. They went from being the world's largest overseas investor to being one of the world's biggest debtors with payments of interest about 40% of all governmental spending. Inflation more than doubled and the value of the Pound Sterling fell about 60%.

The United States stayed out of the war until the last year and a half. While there were losses due to the war the United States suffered far more from a deadly influenza called the "Spanish-flu," which killed far more people than the war. By the time the flu had run its course more than 600,000 people had died. America came out of the war though in great shape economically. It was now ready to take its place in a leadership role among the nations.

Russia was totally altered. It went from being a nominally Christian Monarchy to an atheistic communist dictatorship. This didn't happen suddenly. The seeds of the overthrow of the Monarchy and the establishment of a Communist government grew out of the corruption, callousness, and indifference of the Monarchy and the Church. They did not heed the cries of a people that wanted to be free and to have a voice in government.

The Socialist-Revolutionary Party was established in 1901 and in 1905 the **Russian Revolution** was born. There was a great deal of political unrest throughout vast areas of the Russian Empire. It included terrorism, worker strikes, peasant uprisings, and military mutinies.

Finally Tsar Nicholas II agreed to the creation of a State Duma which was supposed to be a representative advisory body to the Monarchy. When the electorate realized how little power they had actually achieved unrest redoubled and resulted in a general strike in October.

The October Manifesto was presented to the Tsar, which granted basic civil rights and allowed the formation of political parties. It granted the right to vote and established the Duma as the central legislative body. The Tsar waited and argued for three days, but finally signed the manifesto on October 30, 1905.

When the manifesto was proclaimed there were spontaneous demonstrations of support in all the major cities. Unfortunately, the concessions came with renewed, and brutal, action against any unrest. While the Russian liberals were satisfied by the Manifesto, the radical socialists and revolutionaries denounced the elections and called for an armed uprising to "finish off tsarism".

Tsar Nicholas II seems to have had good intentions but made many foolish mistakes. His court was corrupt and lived well while hundreds of thousands of soldiers died needlessly. Bread riots took place followed by Marshal Law and then the Russian Civil War. Three years later the Bolsheviks, led by Lenin and Trotsky, were in full control. Tsar Nicholas and his family were placed under arrest, and on the night of July 16, 1918, Nicholas, his wife, his son, his four daughters, the family's medical doctor, his valet, his wife's lady-in-waiting, and the family cook were all executed.

Famine now stalked the land. In 1921, America sent food to keep millions of Russians from starving to death. In spite of America's help, about 2,000,000 people starved to death. In 1932-1933 another famine arose. This time it was caused by the communist rulers who wanted to collectivize the farms. The Soviet authorities took all the grain and other food from the farmers and left about 10 million people to die of starvation. Another part of Satan's plan had come together.

What the history books conveniently leave out is the part that the Rothschild family and the super rich elite bankers played in the Revolution.

BANKING AND THE RUSSIAN (COMMUNIST) REVOLUTION

It was the financial support from the International Bankers that made the Revolution possible. Why would the bankers want to take part in the Communist Revolution? The answer is two fold.

First, they hated the Russian Tsars and wanted to execute vengeance upon them. Tsar Alexander I had blocked Nathan Mayer Rothschild's world government plan in 1815 at the Congress of Vienna, and later Tsar Alexander II sided with President Abraham Lincoln in 1864. He issued orders that if either England or France actively intervened in the American Civil War, and helped the South; Russia would consider such action a declaration of war and take the side of President Lincoln. To show that he meant business, he sent part of his Pacific Fleet to San Francisco and another part to New York.

The Rothschild's vowed to get even. Now even though Tsar Nicholas II had abdicated the throne over a year before, he, his entire family and servants were stabbed and shot to death.

The second reason they financed the revolution was to keep the nations in a state of tension. That way, they could play off one nation against another. For centuries now the bankers have fomented war, so they could lend to both sides, have them in their debt, collect interest and control them.

Yet, it seems strange that some of the richest men in the world would back communism. Why would they back a system that vowed to destroy capitalism -- the very system that had made them wealthy?

Researcher Gary Allen explained it this way:

> "If one understands that socialism is not a share-the-wealth program, but is in reality a method to consolidate and control the wealth, then the seeming paradox of super-rich men promoting socialism becomes no paradox at all. Instead, it becomes logical, even the perfect tool for power-seeking megalomaniacs. Communism or more accurately, socialism, is not a movement of the downtrodden masses, but of the economic elite."

Gold was shipped by the banks from the United States to Germany for the purpose of securing a train on which Vladimir Lenin and his Bolshevik associates traveled from Germany to Petrograd, Russia, in April 1917. German officials helped arrange for Lenin to pass through their territory, hoping that his activities would weaken Russia or even lead to Russia's withdrawal from the war. German officials however, made a stipulation. They would have to travel to Russia in a sealed train: Germany would not take the chance that he would foment revolution in Germany.

Three years after the start of World War I, the Russian Revolution toppled the Czar. Jacob Schiff of Kuhn, Loeb & Company bragged on his deathbed that he had spent $20 million towards the defeat of the Czar.

The truth though was that much of that money actually funded the communist coup d'état replacing the democratically elected Kerensky regime, which had replaced the Czar months earlier.

The bankers however did not just give this gold away. They wanted to be paid back. In 1920, three gold shipments from Lenin to Kuhn, Loeb & Company and Morgan Guaranty Trust were made to repay $20 million to the bankers.

Strange as it may seem, the Rothschild's financed Communism. They paid Karl Marx to write Das Kapital and they later financed both the Russian Revolution and the Chinese Revolution. Furthermore, certain Western Banks continued to operate openly in the Soviet Union.

On February 8, 1920, an article appeared in the **"Illustrated Sunday Herald"**, written by Winston Churchill.

> "From the days of Illuminati leader Weishaupt, to those of Karl Marx, to those of Trotsky, this worldwide conspiracy has been steadily growing.
>
> And now at last this band of extraordinary personalities from the underworld of the great cities of Europe and America, have gripped the Russian people by the hair of their heads and become the undisputed masters of that enormous empire."

THE FOUNDING OF THE COUNCIL OF FOREIGN RELATIONS (CFR)

In 1921, Bernard Baruch and Colonel Edward Mandell House set up the Council of Foreign Relations. Jacob Schiff ordered them to do so before his death in 1920. This organization was set up for the purpose of consolidating the power of the Rothschilds and the ruling elite in America. One of the most important things for them to do was to make sure that the United States elects the type of President and Congress that would be willing to support the interests of the Rothschild conspiracy.

The CFR membership started out with approximately 1,000 people. This membership included the heads of virtually every industrial empire in America, all the American based international bankers, and the heads of all their tax free foundations.

CONTROL OF THE MEDIA BY THE CFR

The CFR's first job was to gain control of the press. If they could control the information people received and slant it just right, people would respond the way they wanted them to. The CFR would ridicule and try to discredit any news media that would not cooperate.

This task was given to John D. Rockefeller to set up a number of national news magazines such as Life, and Time. He also provided the money for Samuel Newhouse to buy the most prominent and influential newspapers all across the country. Eugene Meyer also sought to buy the Washington Post, Newsweek and the Weekly Magazine. The CFR also needed to gain control of radio, television and the movie industry. This job was given to the international bankers Kuhn Loeb, Goldman Sachs, the Warburgs and the Lehmannns.

THE PROGRESSIVE MOVEMENT

The Progressive Movement was composed mainly of a post-Civil War generation that had grown up in Christian homes in an age of Darwinism and great industrial expansion. They still wanted to retain their Christian morality and do good things, although many of them had lost the faith of their fathers. They strove to bring about reforms and changes in both the social and business environments.

The main thrust of the Progressives was from 1900 to 1920. Three Progressive Presidents were elected during that time: Theodore Roosevelt, a Republican; William Howard Taft, a Republican; and Woodrow Wilson, a Democrat. Roosevelt is particularly noted for Anti-trust laws, Conservation and National Parks. Taft pursued a policy of vigorous judicial progressivism in his efforts to break up trusts, strengthen the Interstate Commerce Commission, and to give more power to the courts. Woodrow Wilson is noted for signing the Federal Reserve Act, the pursuit of peace during WWI, and the League of Nations.

Progressives supported anti-trust laws, the Federal Reserve System, lower tariffs, the Income Tax, the right of women to vote, child labor laws, welfare, and the prohibition of alcoholic beverages.

Some of the things the Progressives tried to do were good. Some had both good and bad features. Some brought about terrible consequences, but all of them were an encroachment of central governmental power over the people.

The Constitution of the United States had established a Republic, but the Progressives wanted to turn the country into a Democracy. The Founders of America had been diametrically opposed to this because they realized that every Democracy in history had always degenerated into mob rule and corruption.

Woodrow Wilson didn't believe that there should be any restrictions on the power of government. He said, "Men as communities are supreme over men as individuals." He also said that there is no essential difference between democracy and socialism. This is an example of the kind of wrong thinking that Satan would use to advance his agenda.

The first stage of Progressivism ended about 1920 but their ideas did not They continued with Franklin Roosevelt's New Deal, Truman's Fair Deal, Lyndon Johnson's Great Society, and now Barak Obama's agenda of National Socialism. In Germany National Socialism was abbreviated to form the letters NAZI.

Contemporary progressives continue to embrace the idea that the government should use its power for the "good of the people" instead of the rights of the individual. They are still pushing their brand of Social Justice. In order for them to achieve their purpose, they have to first destroy the Constitution and discredit the idea that our rights come from God instead of men. The names of some Progressives we are familiar with today are Barack Obama, Hillary Clinton, John McCain, Al Franken, Nancy Pelosi, Harry Reid, John Edwards, Ralph Nader, and Howard Dean.

PROGRESSIVE EDUCATION

Progressive Education was an outgrowth of the Progressive Movement. Progressives thought that education should embrace training in industry, agriculture, and home making. The also wanted to use new techniques to teach reading, writing, math, history, and geography. They thought that children would learn better by experiencing those things in which they were interested. The progressives insisted, therefore, that education be based on activity directed by the child. A typical progressive slogan was "Learn by Doing!"

One of the early proponents of progressive education was John Dewey. He was a Philosopher, Psychologist, and

Educator. He conducted educational experiments and wrote extensively on the subject. He has been called the father of Progressive Education.

While some of the thoughts and techniques of the progressive educators had merit, some of their techniques didn't work very well; such as "the look-say" method of learning to read. Progressive Education was based on the Darwinian principle that children are nothing more **than highly evolved social animals.**

In March 1925, the Tennessee legislature passed a measure known as the Butler Act. This law required public schools to only teach the biblical account of creation as fact. This law made it illegal to teach Darwin's theory of evolution as a fact.

The American Civil Liberties Union (ACLU), advertised in Tennessee newspapers to find some one willing to challenge the Butler Act. John T. Scopes, a substitute high school biology teacher, volunteered. Scopes was promptly cited for teaching evolution as a fact in his biology class, which set the stage for what was then termed "the trial of the century". Press representatives from most of the nation's major newspapers poured into Dayton and a circus-like atmosphere prevailed.

The judge made clear to the jury that the law's constitutionality or efforts to support the validity of Darwin's theory were not at issue. The only question was whether or not Scopes had presented evolution as fact and for that he was found guilty and fined $100.

While the State of Tennessee won the lawsuit, they lost the public relations battle. The damage had been done. Other states did not want to pass similar laws and have to endure the same notoriety and ridicule as Tennessee. This opened the door to teaching evolution as a fact in all the public schools. In 1967, the Butler Act was repealed.

John Dewey and others saw children as social animals that were to be trained to take their proper place in society. When we consider that John Dewey was one of the 34 signers of the Humanist Manifesto of 1934, it becomes abundantly clear the direction that Progressive Education would take.

HUMANIST MANIFESTO OF 1934

FIRST: Religious humanists regard the universe as self-existing and not created.

SECOND: Humanism believes that man is a part of nature and that he has emerged as a result of a continuous process.

THIRD: Holding an organic view of life, humanists find that the traditional dualism of mind and body must be rejected.

FOURTH: Humanism recognizes that man's religious culture and civilization, as clearly depicted by anthropology and history, are the product of a gradual development due to his interaction with his natural environment and with his social heritage. The individual born into a particular culture is largely molded by that culture.

FIFTH: Humanism asserts that the nature of the universe depicted by modern science makes unacceptable any supernatural or cosmic guarantees of human values. Obviously humanism does not deny the possibility of realities as yet undiscovered, but it does insist that the way to determine the existence and value of any and all realities is by means of intelligent inquiry and by the assessment of their relations to human needs. Religion must formulate its hopes and plans in the light of the scientific spirit and method.

SIXTH: We are convinced that the time has passed for theism, deism, modernism, and the several varieties of "new thought".

SEVENTH: Religion consists of those actions, purposes, and experiences which are humanly significant. Nothing human is alien to the religious. It includes labor, art, science, philosophy, love, friendship, recreation -- all that is in its degree expressive of intelligently satisfying human living. The distinction between the sacred and the secular can no longer be maintained.

EIGHTH: Religious Humanism considers the complete realization of human personality to be the end of man's life and seeks its development and fulfillment in the here and now. This is the explanation of the humanist's social passion.

NINTH: In the place of the old attitudes involved in worship and prayer the humanist finds his religious emotions expressed in a heightened sense of personal life and in a cooperative effort to promote social well-being.

TENTH: It follows that there will be no uniquely religious emotions and attitudes of the kind hitherto associated with belief in the supernatural.

ELEVENTH: Man will learn to face the crises of life in terms of his knowledge of their naturalness and probability. Reasonable and manly attitudes will be fostered by education and supported by custom. We assume that humanism will take the path of social and mental hygiene and discourage sentimental and unreal hopes and wishful thinking.

TWELFTH: Believing that religion must work increasingly for joy in living, religious humanists aim to foster the creative in man and to encourage achievements that add to the satisfactions of life.

THIRTEENTH: Religious humanism maintains that all associations and institutions exist for the fulfillment of human life. The intelligent evaluation, transformation, control, and direction of such associations and institutions with a view to the enhancement of human life is the purpose and program of humanism. Certainly religious institutions, their ritualistic forms, ecclesiastical methods, and communal activities must be reconstituted as rapidly as experience allows, in order to function effectively in the modern world.

FOURTEENTH: The humanists are firmly convinced that existing acquisitive and profit-motivated society has shown itself to be inadequate and that a radical change in methods, controls, and motives must be instituted. A socialized and cooperative economic order must be established to the end that the equitable distribution of the means of life be possible. The goal of humanism is a free and universal society in which people voluntarily and intelligently cooperate for the common good. Humanists demand a shared life in a shared world.

FIFTEENTH AND LAST: We assert that humanism will: (a) affirm life rather than deny it; (b) seek to elicit the possibilities of life, not flee from them; and (c) endeavor to establish the conditions of a satisfactory life for all, not merely for the few. By this positive morale and intention humanism will be guided, and from this perspective and alignment the techniques and efforts of humanism will flow.

Humanism follows Darwin's theory of evolution and considers man as nothing more than an intelligent animal. This manifesto clearly rejects the God of the Bible and all Christian morality. While the manifesto does not call for the complete elimination of religion, it wants to completely restructure it.

Progressive educators applying this humanistic view quickly begin to implement their philosophy in the classrooms. Of course this had to be done gradually. First they would have to train the teachers. To accomplish this they would have to get their ideas accepted in the universities. That would take several generations. Only then would they be able to bring all their ideas into the classroom. Their goal was to remake society. This would take time and they would need to exercise great patience.

John Dewey, as a University Professor of Education and Psychology wrote books to instruct teachers on how they should teach. In this way his influence is still being felt in teacher colleges and public school classrooms all over the country. These new teachers would need new teaching materials. The old textbooks would not do because their goal was to restructure society.

Progressive educators wanted to teach a new morality based on evolution therefore it did not suit their purpose that the students should learn that the signers of the Declaration of Independence and the Constitution were for the most part devoted Christians and many of them were Christian

Ministers. They would need to downplay this. They couldn't change the history books too fast though because the older teachers and the children's parents might become alarmed and reject them. First they would deemphasize the Christian Founding of our country by leaving out important facts. Then they would claim that not all of the founders were Christian. Some were Deists. Eventually they would try to completely hide the role Christianity played in the founding of the United States and its Constitution.

After several generations most Americans are ignorant of the historical Christian foundation of America's documents and institutions. They also now believe the lie that the First Amendment of the Constitution requires the separation of Church and State. This is the exact opposite of the intentions of those who framed and signed the Constitution.

> David Barton has done a tremendous amount of research regarding America's founding and history. He has produced great books, videos, and resources for anyone who is interested in the real history and heritage of America. Check out his website:
>
> HTTP://WWW.WALLBUILDERS.COM/

Since Progressive Humanists do not accept the God of the Bible, the morality of the Bible is not acceptable either. Therefore, they began to teach that there is no authority for anyone to say something is right or wrong. Right and wrong will now be determined by what the majority thinks. In 1962-63 they were able to obtain several US Supreme Court decisions which suppressed the reading of the Bible and prayer in the public schools.

Since most Americans have been convinced that the Constitution calls for the separation of Church and State nearly all vestiges of Christianity have been removed from the public schools. Now they can bring in other things; such as yoga, witchcraft, Indian Mysticism, and in the name of Diversity they can even teach Islam. Anything now goes in the public schools except Christianity and Judeo-Christian ethics.

Progressive Humanists almost have it their way, but some Christians have begun to object to the things that are happening in the public schools. Some of them have started home schooling their children or sending them to religious private schools. These parents actually believe that children are a heritage from the Lord. Progressive Humanists consider them a real danger to their plans and are trying to find ways to combat it.. Germany and several other countries are now trying to put a stop to home-schooling and are also working to get the private religious schools closed. They do not consider children to be a heritage from the Lord entrusted to their parents. Instead they are considered to be "Property of the State". They want to mold the children to fit their world view, not that of their parents. The battle that is now going on in the field of education has nothing to do with either quality of education or money. It is instead a battle for the minds and hearts of the children. Who will influence and mold the children; their parents or the State? This kind of thinking has also come to the United States.

THE ROARING TWENTIES

After the First World War, people wanted to get their lives in order. They wanted things to go back to normal, but many new things were happening. Electric lights, power and telephone lines were spreading across the country. Indoor plumbing and modern sewer systems were also being installed.

Henry Ford was making the Model T using the assembly line which lowered the cost. This made it possible for more people to own an automobile. There was the excitement of the movies (silent), and radio drama. Louis Armstrong and Duke Ellington created the "Jazz Age". Adding to the excitement, Charles Lindbergh flew the first non-stop flight across the Atlantic, and Babe Ruth hit 60 homeruns in 1927. People were dancing the Charleston and makeup for women became fashionable.

The 1920's were a feel good era but not everything was sweetness and light. In 1919, the Progressives lobbied with Church organizations in order to combat the evils of alcohol abuse. The result was the 18th Amendment of the Constitution which prohibited the manufacture, sale, or import of alcoholic beverages. This was a terrible mistake however, because outlawing alcohol did not stop its use or abuse. It only drove it underground. A whole new industry sprang up with hundreds of illegal stills, Al Capone, speakeasies, and gangsters. Crime rates soared, gangsters made millions of dollars and law enforcement agencies were corrupted. It didn't take very many years for people to realize their mistake, and it was finally repealed by the 21st Amendment in 1933.

BANKING AND THE GREAT DEPRESSION

The Federal Reserve was set up for the very purpose of enabling a few super rich and powerful people who owned the banks to gain complete control over the money system. After the Federal Reserve was formed in 1913 they immediately sought to bring the United States into the First World War. As far as the banks were concerned this was something they considered to be a top priority, because when a nation is at war it spends a lot of money. Where will it get this money? It will borrow from the banks, of course. At first the banks were not very successful getting the United States into the war. The American people wanted nothing to do with the war but after enough strings were pulled America finally became a part of the First World War in April of 1917.

The Bible says, **Proverbs 22:7 *"the rich rule over the poor, and the borrower is servant to the lender"***. That is how the US Government became the servant of the banks.

When the war was over, there was a spirit of optimism in America, and the banks were ready to cash in on it. They lowered the interest rates and made cash available for loans. Lots of money eventually went into the stock market where people were able to buy stock with very low margins. In 1929, right before the stock market crash, margin requirements were only 10%. Stock brokers would loan $9.00 to buy stock for every dollar the investor deposited with the broker. Since it was so easy to buy lots of stock with very little money and since the market was constantly going up, great profits could be made with very little investment. The problem however is that it wasn't really investment, it was speculation. As long as prices continued to go up everything would be fine but what if prices started to go down? The stock brokers would demand all the borrowed money used to buy the stocks to be repaid immediately.

Stock prices were already far higher than could be justified. There was no way that anyone could hope to receive a decent return on their money through company profits. The stock market was being fed by speculator greed on the basis of the greater fool theory. The greater fool theory is this: "I know that the stock is too high but the market is going up, so

I will continue to buy stocks and then sell them to a greater fool than I am." But then on Tuesday, October 29, 1929 it happened. The stock started down. All the speculators now wanted to sell to the greater fool but they couldn't find any. No one wanted to buy. The market quickly crashed. Thousands of speculators, Wall Street brokers, and banks were wiped out. It was reported that people jumped out of windows in their despair.

Two months after the original crash in October, stockholders had lost more than $40 billion dollars. By the end of 1930, the stock market had begun to regain some of its losses, but it was not enough to keep America from entering what is now called The Great Depression.

The crashing of the stock market began a chain reaction of economic consequences. Since the investors and speculators could not repay the money they had borrowed to buy stocks, brokerage houses and banks began to fail. This caused depositors to become alarmed. They feared that their money might not be safe so they tried to withdraw their deposits. Even good banks now began to fail. Under the reserve banking system, banks are able to lend out about ten times as much money as they have on deposit. That system seems to work just fine until people want to withdraw their deposits. When that happens the money is not there to repay them. During the 1930's over 9,000 banks failed.

When people default on loans, the money that was created out of nothing in order to create the loan simply vanishes. The banks then suffer loss and often fail, taking the depositor's money with them.

When people do not have the money to spent, merchandise sits on the shelves, stores do not reorder, factories quit producing and lay off employees. (Unemployment rose to 25 %.) The former employees have no money to spend and the whole process starts over, while the problems grow larger.

There had been recessions in the United States before. Some of them were the natural processes of growth and contraction during the business cycle. During these recessions weak business and banks were quickly eliminated. Debt was cancelled and the economy soon recovered.

Other recessions were deliberately brought on by the central banks because of their greed and lust for power. These recessions also ended when the banks got what they wanted. What happened in 1929 and the years following was no ordinary recession. It soon became known as the Great Depression.

This Depression was brought on by America's Central Bank, the Federal Reserve and by the super elite. It did not occur by accident or because of stupidity. It was done on purpose to accomplish the goals of the elite.

THE SUPER ELITE – WHO ARE THEY? WHAT ARE THEY TRYING TO DO?

We will discuss who the Super Elite are in greater detail when we come the Twenty First Century but for now we will simply state that there are several layers of the Super Elite. The lowest groups include non governmental groups such as the National and World Federation of Churches, Educators, Teachers Unions, Unions, and Masons as well as many other groups too numerous to mention. Next are people who belong to elite groups from which Congressmen, Presidents, and rulers are selected, like the Council on Foreign Relations, the Trilateral Commission, and the Round Table in England. Next on the list is the Bilderberg Group. They hold conferences once a year to decide the future of the world. They consist of about 100 to 130 of the super elite from many different countries. Next are the front men. They are usually not in government themselves but they are the ones who pull the strings of those in government. In the 1930's it was people like John D. Rockefeller, J. P. Morgan, and other bankers who used money donated to political campaigns in order to pass legislation they wanted. The upper echelons of the super elite were powerful European Bankers with the Rothschild family at the top of the heap, just under Satan himself.

AMERICAN STRUGGLES TO GET RID OF THE DEPRESSION

Congress was alarmed because of all the businesses that were failing; so in 1930 they created the Smoot-Hawley Tariff which charged a high tax for imports. This resulted in far less trade and provoked retaliation by other countries which passed their own Tariff laws.

In 1933 there was a new President, Franklin D. Roosevelt. He would pursue the Progressive, Socialist agenda of Woodrow Wilson with a vengeance. He wasted no time. On March 6, 1933 he declared a four day national bank holiday to prevent anyone from exporting or hoarding gold or silver. Then on March 9th, the Emergency Banking Act was passed. This act forced banks to allow the government to inspect them before they reopened. It gave the government power to close down banks and reorganize banks that were salvageable.

April 5th, the President issued an order making it illegal to hoard gold coins, gold bullion or gold certificates. Violation of this order was punishable by a $10,000 fine or 10 years in prison. Eventually, gold coins from 1933 and earlier were exempted from this rule so coin collectors could avoid prosecution.

On June 5, 1933, the United States abandoned the gold standard. All existing contracts and currency that required redemption in gold were no longer considered valid for United States citizens. However gold was still used to settle international debts, and people in foreign countries could redeem their dollars at the rate of $35 for an ounce of pure gold.

The Banking Act of June 16, 1933 created the Federal Deposit Insurance Corporation, better known as the FDIC. It was set up to insure deposits in banks up to $2500. In today's money that would be about $150,000. The purpose was to instill trust in the banking system.

As the depression deepened, there was plenty of everything except money. Without money, people couldn't buy. The stores couldn't sell. The factories could not continue to operate. The unemployment rolls swelled to 25%. People were homeless and had to stand in long lines to receive a little bread and soup. This condition continued month after month and year after year.

Many things were tried to remedy the situation. Farmers could not continue to grow crops that sold for less than the cost of production so they began to pour out their milk, burn their wheat and destroy their crops in order to try to raise prices through scarcity. The government also went along with that idea. They passed legislation and regulations to limit the amount of acreage that could be planted of various crops.

This was all based on the false theory that the problem was that there were too many goods. The truth is that there was not too much food, clothing, houses, cars, or radios. There just wasn't enough money to buy them. The government took all their gold and banks wouldn't lend money for people to buy and for factories to operate.

The government also tried other things to get the economy going - like building dams, parks, public works and buildings. This did give some people at least a temporary paycheck.

Most of the things the government did actually prolonged the depression. The Great Depression did not end until the beginning of World War II. When America began to gear up for war. Suddenly the banks now had plenty of money to lend.

Before we leave this era we need to note the Social Security Act which President Roosevelt signed into law August 14, 1935.

On top of everything else there was a great drought in the Mississippi Valley, and parts of Oklahoma and Kansas became dust bowls. People could not pay their taxes or other debts. Many of them just packed up their vehicles with whatever they could carry with them and left everything else behind. Lots of them migrated to California. This was the basis of John Steinbeck's book, "The Grapes of Wrath," which was also made into a movie.

EVALUATION OF THE FIRST PART OF THE 20TH CENTURY

The first part of the 20th century was filled with new and exciting things. An explosion of inventions was about to take place. People who grew up riding on horses and in buggies would soon be riding in automobiles and listening to the radio. During this time, electrical power grids stretched across the country. Television was invented and moving pictures became the new entertainment. Not all the changes, however, were good.

Religion and morals definitely took a turn for the worse. Evolution was now being taught in the schools. The roaring 20s were characterized by loose morals, and the churches were losing their saltiness.

The rationalistic philosophies and theology being taught in European seminaries was now coming to America. In order to gain academic prestige and credentials, Theological Seminaries in America started sending their professors to study in Europe. When these professors came back home, they brought with them the rationalistic liberal theology of Europe, and began teaching it to their students. As a result, many churches began to have pastors who did not believe that the Bible was God's word, that Jesus was born of a virgin or that the miracles of the Bible actually happened. They began to preach a social gospel, instead of teaching the good news of our salvation through faith in Jesus Christ.

The good news is that even though many preachers no longer believed the Bible, the members of their churches did. They continued to practice the things they had been taught. If that had not been true, the Great Depression may have turned into a time of social unrest and revolution. Even so, the Progressives, Socialists, and Communists gained great power at this time.

During the first part of the 20th century Satan had been laying the foundation for things he had planned for the future. His banking agents had taken over the money supply. The schools had started using teaching methods which fit in with progressive, evolutionary philosophy. History books were also being changed so that children would have less appreciation for their God-given freedoms granted under the Constitution of the United States.

In spite of all that Satan had been able to do, most Americans still believed in God and put their trust in Him. They still sent out missionaries to bring others to Christ. There were still Christian seminaries and faithful Pastors who taught God's Word.

Satan had not been able to do all that he wanted, but he had put in place many things to undermine the foundations of America. He had his people high up in the American government. Communism had been established and had already killed and imprisoned millions of Christians. He would continue to try to obtain a one-world monetary system and world government. His goal was to bring the whole world under his control so that they might now worship him instead of God.

CHAPTER 13

THE TWENTIETH CENTURY (1941-1960) WORLD WAR II

W orld War II began when Germany invaded Poland in 1939 and ended in 1945 after the United States had dropped two atomic bombs on cities in Japan. It was an international conflict mainly between the **Axis Powers** – Germany Italy, and Japan - and the **Allied Powers** – France, Britain, and the United States, the Soviet Union and China. It resulted in more loss of life and material destruction than any other war in recorded history.

Since this is not intended to be a history book, we will not go into detail regarding the war. Instead we will concentrate on why the war occurred and the results of the war.

The seeds of the war were sown by France and Great Britain at the end of World War I. France and Britain wanted to make the Germans pay for the war. The only way Germany could pay was to print money. These printed pieces of paper soon became worthless and resulted in the collapse of the democratic government in Germany. This opened the way for the dictatorship under Adolph Hitler.

Hitler belonged to the Nazi (National Socialist) Party. If you consider Communism as Socialism of the far left, then Nazism can be considered as Socialism of the far right.

The Nazis believed in the supremacy of an Aryan master race and claimed that the German people were the purest Aryan nation. They claimed that the Jews were the greatest threat to the Aryan race and German nation. They considered Jews parasites.

The Nazis also wanted to rescue Germany from trying to pay reparations from World War I. This had brought on hyper-inflation. They promoted a managed economy which was a nationalistic form of socialism. They supported social welfare programs, a just wage for workers, and protection from capitalist exploitation.

Hitler wanted Germany to bring about the Third Reich. The Third Reich was to be a restoration of the Roman Empire which would reign for a thousand years. In the mid-1930s Hitler began secretly to rearm Germany. They intended to grab the land and resources that they needed by force. In 1938, he sent troops to occupy Austria and then in 1939 he annexed Czechoslovakia. On Sept. 1, 1939 Germany invaded Poland. Two days later France and Britain declared war on Germany. In April 1940 Germany overwhelmed Denmark and began its conquest of Norway. In May German forces swept through The Netherlands and Belgium and began their invasion of France.

Germany then began bombing raids on Britain in preparation for an invasion, but after strong British resistance Hitler postponed the invasion indefinitely.

In the mean time, back in the United States, the American people didn't want anything to do with the war. The powers that be and the moneyed elite were no doubt getting a little nervous about now. It looked like Hitler might conquer all of Europe. He had to be stopped. President Roosevelt could not declare war himself. Only Congress could do that. Therefore, it would require something to happen which would motivate the American people to support the war.

In 1941, President Roosevelt found a way to bring America into the war. Japan had been at war with China for some time and had allied itself with Germany. Japan had been buying scrap steel and oil from the United States. Roosevelt refused to sell any more scrap steel or oil. Japan was totally dependent upon the United States for both. He knew that this would provoke the Japanese to attack America.

On December 7, 1941, the Japanese bombed Pearl Harbor in Hawaii. They almost took out the Pacific Fleet. The sailors were, for the most part, on shore leave. When the Japanese bombers arrived there wasn't anyone to mount the guns and fire back.

Messages were intercepted to indicate that the Japanese were going to attack. These messages were sent to Washington but supposedly Roosevelt didn't receive them until after the attack. The Naval Commanders were not warned. The attack was devastating and all of America was shaken. Roosevelt immediately goes to Congress and asks for a Declaration of War against Japan. Congress obliges. The Axis Powers then declared war on the United States.

All of America was now put on a war footing. Soldiers were being drafted. Industry began gearing up to make machines of war. Women were given jobs in the Defense Industry turning out ships, airplanes, and tanks. Everything people used was also being rationed, such as: meat, sugar, coffee, tea, tires and gasoline. The speed limit was reduced to 35 mph to conserve rubber and gasoline.

The banks that didn't have any money to lend in order to help get the economy moving now suddenly had lots of money to promote the war effort. America was totally committed to the production of an incredible number of planes, tanks, trucks and ships.

The Allies first confronted the Axis Powers in North Africa and Egypt. They continued by invading Italy and pushing on North to the German defense line. On June 6, 1944 the Western Allies invaded southern France while Russia came from the North.

On February 4-11, 1945, a very important meeting occurred. President Franklin Roosevelt of the United States, Prime Minister Winston Churchill of Great Britain, and Joseph Stalin of the Soviet Union met together. This meeting was called the Yalta Conference and took place in Russia. In this conference, the three leaders decided how to slice and dice up the countries of Europe and how they would occupy Germany. Plans were also being made to establish the United Nations after the end of the war.

They decided to divide up Germany into three occupation zones, one for the Soviet Union, one for Great Britain, and one for the United States. Later on the United States and Great Britain gave France part of their zone to occupy. The capital of Germany, Berlin, was also to be divided up into three zones. This would later become a trouble spot, because people in the Soviet bloc would try to escape by traveling to the Western Zone. To keep their citizens from escaping, the Soviet Union eventually built the Berlin wall.

On May 8, 1945 Germany surrendered. Hitler and his lady companion, Eva Braun, whom he had now married, committed suicide to avoid capture.

In the Pacific the Allies fought many bloody battles to retake the Pacific Islands the Japanese occupied as well as Okinawa. The only thing left to invade was the Japanese mainland. President Roosevelt died of a cerebral hemorrhage and Vice President Harry Truman was now President. President Truman was now faced with a very difficult decision. If he invaded Japan, he would have to be prepared to sacrifice the lives of hundreds of thousands of American soldiers as well as a like number of Japanese soldiers. On the other hand, America now possessed at least two atomic bombs. Even though they were frightful weapons, Truman reasoned that it would be worthwhile to use them and save many lives.

On the morning of August 6, 1945, an atomic bomb named Little Boy was dropped on Hiroshima. Two days later another atomic bomb named Fat Man was dropped on Nagasaki. The bombs killed as many as 140,000 people in Hiroshima and 80,000 in Nagasaki by the end of 1945, with roughly half of those deaths occurring on the days of the bombings. The Japanese agreed to surrender on August 14.

Estimates of the total military and civilian casualties of World War II varied from 35 million to 60 million killed, including about 6 million Jews who died in the Holocaust. Besides the dead, many millions of civilians were wounded and made homeless throughout Europe and East Asia.

THE AFTERMATH OF WAR

As a result of war most of Europe was devastated. The United Nations came into existence on October 24, 1945. Europe was soon divided between the Eastern Bloc dominated by Russia and Western Europe.

The ink was hardly dry on the surrender documents before mounting tensions between the United States and the Soviet Union finally evolved into the formation of the American-led NATO and the Soviet led Warsaw Pact.

By the end of the war, the European economy had collapsed with 70% of the industrial infrastructure destroyed. Hunger and poverty stalked Europe. American leaders feared that poverty and hunger would make West European countries vulnerable to communism. Secretary of State George C. Marshall came up with a plan to rebuild Europe and stomp out poverty and hunger.

The Marshall plan was a great success. Between 1948 and 1952, $13.5 billion worth of aid was given to 17 countries, including West Germany, and resulted in a 25% increase in their gross national product.

COMMUNIST ACTIVITY IN THE UNITED STATES GOVERNMENT

In 1948, the House Un-American Activities Committee heard testimony from former spy and former editor of Time magazine Whittaker Chambers that numerous people working in the federal government were in fact communist agents. Some of the people Chambers named had already died or left the country. Others refused to answer questions, citing the Fifth Amendment. Alger Hiss was one of those accused. He denied all charges but was later proved to be a communist.

Sen. Joseph McCarthy charged that there were many communists and seven Soviet spies inside the federal government. He also claimed that there were many communists in the movie industry as well as other high positions in society. Sen. McCarthy was ridiculed, and the term McCarthyism came into being. McCarthyism was a term soon applied to all who engaged in anti-Communist activities. The truth is that there were plenty of Communists in government and for those who have sought the truth, McCarthy has been vindicated.

Communists came into government during the 1930s. President Roosevelt was a progressive Socialist and he placed many progressives, socialists and communists in the government.

There are many different brands of socialism. There are the progressives, like Theodore Roosevelt and Woodrow Wilson. There is National Socialism, like Germany had. They were called Nazis. There are Fascists, like Mussolini in Italy. There are Fabian socialists, like in England and communists as in Russia. While there are differences between them, they are all socialists. When it suits them, they work together. When it doesn't suit them, they oppose each other.

What McCarthy said was correct. The State Department was full of Communists, many of whom were spying for the Soviet Union. When Pres. Harry Truman assumed office he may have been unaware of how many communists were actually in government.

President Truman appeared to be a Christian, and a very honorable, honest and patriotic American. He stood firm against communism, but in one particular case. I believe that he was misled by Communists in the State Department without realizing it. Several things happened during his administration that was disastrous.

CHINA FALLS TO COMMUNISM

The United States betrayed China. During World War II, China had been our friend and ally. China had been fighting

Japan already for a number of years before we got into the war because Japan had invaded Manchuria, a province of China, in 1931. At this time China was not only fighting against Japan, but it was also struggling against the Chinese Communists who were trying to take over. During World War II we provided aid, arms and ammunition to help China fight against Japan; but now after the War, our government looked at things differently.

Chiang Kai-shek the president of Nationalist China, had not only been a friend of the United States, but was also a Christian. China was on the verge of defeating the communists and opening up China to Christianity, capitalism and freedom. The United States and China could have remained friends and allies all these years, but that was not to be.

President Truman, on the advice of people who have been proven to be communists in the State Department and those behind the scenes who were pulling the strings, cut off all aid to Chiang Kai-shek. Without ammunition and supplies, his army could not continue to fight. Therefore he took what was left of his army and retreated to Taiwan. The communist "People's Republic of China" was set up on main land China in 1949 and they claim that Taiwan also belongs to them. They have threatened to invade Taiwan and take it by force but the United States has acted as Taiwan's protector. So far, China has been kept at bay and has not tried to carry out their threats

Those pulling the strings, particularly the international bankers could now rejoice. They had achieved their goals. Now they had an enemy set up for the United States so that they could continue to lend money for arms and war.

Since President Truman pulled the rug out from under Chiang Kai-shek and paved the way for the communists to take over it would not be long till he might have regretted it. The very next year, in June of 1950, communist North Korea invaded South Korea.

THE KOREAN WAR

President Truman foolishly made great concessions to Joseph Stalin of Russia in their meeting at the Potsdam conference without consulting the Koreans. They divided up Korea along the 38th parallel with Russia occupying the northern half and the United States occupying the southern half of the country.

These nations were only supposed to be occupied until they could have elections and set up their own governments. The communists had other ideas. Failure was almost guaranteed.

On June 25, 1950, North Korea attacked South Korea and almost completely overran it. Pres. Truman had drastically cut the military after the war. There were very few American troops in Korea when the North attacked, but there were a number of troops in Japan. They were quickly sent to Korea.

In the United States, the war was officially described as a police action by the United Nations. Moreover, because it was considered a police action, the U. S. Congress never issued a declaration of war. The fact of the matter was that most of the fighting and dying was done by the United States military.

After reinforcements from Japan arrived, the war could have been won for the South if communist China had not sent in men and materials to fight against the South and the Soviet Union provided air support for the North Koreans.

Gen. MacArthur wanted to win the war by bombing the supply lines out of China, but Pres. Truman was afraid that this would bring Russia and China fully into the war. Pres. Truman eventually fired and replaced Gen. MacArthur because of the disagreement.

From the beginning of the war until the armistice was signed on July 27, 1953, almost 37,000 American soldiers had died. If President Truman had not betrayed Chiang Kai-shek, Communist China would not have been fighting in Korea and many American soldiers would not have died.

PRESIDENT DWIGHT D. EISENHOWER (1953-1960)

Dwight D. Eisenhower became president, right before the end of the Korean War. He had been the supreme commander of the troops invading France during World War II. When he ran for president, the slogan of his supporters was, "I like Ike."

Eisenhower believed in achieving peace through strength. In 1953, the signing of a truce in Korea brought about an armed peace along the border of South Korea.

In his domestic policy, the president pursued a middle course, continuing most of the new deal and fair deal programs. He supported desegregation of schools and the Armed Forces. He wrote, "There must be no second class citizens in this country."

Eisenhower, a man of war, was also a man of peace. His administration was the most peaceful and prosperous of the 20th century.

I believe the decade of the 1950's to be the happiest and most prosperous decade in the history of America. This was the decade of John Dean, Elvis Presley, romantic movies and music. Businesses hummed, production skyrocketed and generally people were very optimistic and happy. Alas, this happy period was not to last.

THE NATION OF ISRAEL

On May 14, 1948, after almost 2000 years, the nation of Israel was reborn. After the people of Israel were forcibly removed by the Romans from their land, they were scattered all over the world, but they never lost their identity. Wherever they went they remained a separate people. They were often discriminated against, persecuted, and denied the ability to enter into certain crafts, trades, and guilds. Therefore, they entered into fields where they were very successful, such as banking, trading and medicine.

The Jewish people had suffered terrible persecutions by the Catholics in Spain during the Middle Ages and more recently by the pogroms in Russia. These persecutions led many Jews to consider the possibility of reestablishing themselves in an independent nation. In 1897, the first Zionist Congress decided to try to establish a home for the Jewish people in Palestine. By this time, a few Jewish settlers had already come to Palestine, bought land, and started farming communities. The main Jewish settlements came to Palestine after the First World War.

One of the main proponents of a Jewish homeland in Palestine was a man by the name of Chaim Azriel Weizmann. He was president of the Zionist organization in Great Britain, and would later become the first president of the state of Israel. He was also a chemist, and he developed a process by which acetone could be made by bacterial fermentation. This was very important because acetone was essential in making high explosives needed for the war effort against Germany in World War I. Germany had gained control of the ingredients needed to make acetone. Britain was desperate. They had to have acetone to make explosives. Therefore, they were very grateful when Weizmann came up with a way for them to make acetone.

Wiseman had a long-time relationship with Lloyd-George who was also the Minister of Munitions at the time of the explosives crisis. Toward the end of the war, Lloyd-George was prime minister of Great Britain. When Wiseman was asked how he could be rewarded for his contribution to the British war effort, he replied that he wanted nothing for himself. He just wanted a homeland for the Jews.

Now, at Baron Walter Rothschild's request, the British Cabinet met, after which foreign Sec. Arthur James Balfour would send a letter to Baron Rothschild. This letter would soon become known as the Balfour mandate.

Foreign Office, November 2nd, 1917.

Dear Lord Rothschild,

I have much pleasure in conveying to you, on behalf of His Majesty's Government, the following declaration of sympathy with Jewish Zionist aspirations which has been submitted to, and approved by, the Cabinet: "HisMajesty'sGovernmentviewwithfavourtheestablishment in Palestine of a national home for the Jewish people, and will use their best endeavours to facilitate the achievement of this object, it being clearly understood that nothing shall be done which may prejudice the civil and religious rights of existing non-Jewish communities in Palestine, or the rights and political status enjoyed by Jews in any other country". I should be grateful if you would bring this declaration to the knowledge of the Zionist Federation.

Yours sincerely
Arthur James Balfour

Soon after the Balfour Mandate, Field Marshall Edmund Allenby would be approaching Jerusalem. Allenby was a British soldier and he had been made commander of the Egyptian Expeditionary Force. His job was to take back territory from the Turkish Ottoman Empire. By December 1917, he had made his way to Jerusalem. Allenby had great respect for the city of Jerusalem and wanted to preserve it from destruction. Therefore he sent airplanes to drop leaflets over the city. The leaflets urged the people to surrender, and he signed his name Allenby.

The people living in Jerusalem had never seen airplanes before, and when they read the leaflets, they confused Allenby with Allah. They thought the airplanes were heavenly messengers, and that God was telling them to surrender, which they did on December 9, 1917.

On December 11, 1917, Allenby and a few of his staff officers dismounted from their horses in honor of the holy city, and walked into the city through the Jaffa gate, where they were well-received.

After the British conquered the Middle East in 1917, they created two states. One of the states was called Palestine, which included what is now known as Israel, the West Bank, Gaza and Jordan. The other state was called Mesopotamia, which was later renamed Iraq.

Soon Jews immigrated to Palestine, but it wasn't very long before they began to experience Arab resistance. In 1921, there were Arab riots. After the riots, the British authorities enacted a system of immigration quotas.

Jewish immigration grew slowly during the 1920s. It greatly speeded up in the 1930s after Jews in Europe began to experience much greater persecution, especially by Hitler's Germany.

The rapid increase in Jewish migration led to a large-scale Arab rebellion in Palestine. In order to satisfy the Arabs, in 1939, Britain issued what is known as the White Paper. The white paper limited Jewish immigration to 75,000 over the next five years. This broke with the terms of the British mandate, as decreed by the League of Nations and the Balfour declaration. As result, boatloads of Jewish immigrants were returned to Europe, where they were killed by the Nazis.

Between 1939 and 1945, 72% of the Jews in Nazi occupied Europe were murdered. About a fourth of them were children. About half of all European Jews were killed. The Holocaust had a decisive impact not only upon the Jews but also the whole world.

In 1945, at the end of the Second World War, the Jews which had survived in Central Europe were now displaced persons (refugees). A survey showed that 97% of them wanted to immigrate to Palestine. A stream of small boats began carrying stateless Jews to Palestine. The British came against the Holocaust survivors, and tried to keep them from immigrating to Palestine. This led to growing Jewish resistance against the British administration. Finally, Great Britain decided to refer the Palestinian problem to the United Nations.

The UN appointed a committee to decide how to deal with Palestine. They recommended a partition of Palestine in which two states would be created, one Arab, and one Jewish. The city of Jerusalem would be under the direct administration of the United Nations. This was ratified by the UN General Assembly on November 29, 1947. The resolution also called for Britain to evacuate a seaport and help with the Jewish migration. Britain ignored this part of the resolution and continued to stop boats loaded with Jews trying to get to Palestine. They arrested the Jews and imprisoned them in camps on Cyprus.

Britain was afraid that the partition would damage their relations with the Arabs. Therefore, they refused to cooperate with United Nations, even denying the UN access to Palestine.

Fighting between the Arab and Jewish communities begin immediately after the UN decision to create a Jewish state. The Arab states declared that they would greet any attempt to form a Jewish state with war.

The countries of the Arab League planned an invasion of Palestine and the routing of the Jews, as soon as the British completed their withdrawal from Palestine.

On May 14, 1948, the last British forces left Haifa. The Jewish agency led by David Ben-Gurion, declared the creation of the state of Israel, in accordance with the 1947 UN partition plan. Pres. Harry S. Truman of the United States immediately recognized the new state of Israel. This was quickly followed by Joseph Stalin of the Soviet Union also recognizing the state of Israel.

Members of the Arab League (Egypt, Transjordan, Syria, Lebanon, and Iraq) rejected the UN partition decision and declared war against the Jews.

To begin with the Arabs had an advantage, because the British had maintained an embargo which prevented the Jews from importing arms or manpower, while the neighboring Arab states could supply local Arabs with arms. They were, however, coming up against Jews who believed they were fighting for their lives.

In March 1949, after many months of battle, a permanent cease-fire went into effect. By this time Israel had conquered Galilee and the Negev desert.

Following the cease-fire, Britain finally released over 2000 Jewish prisoners it had been holding on Cyprus, and recognized the state of Israel. On May 11, 1949, Israel was admitted as a member of the United Nations.

Out of the Jewish population of 650,000, some 6,000 men and women were killed in the fighting, including 4,000 soldiers. The number of Arab losses was estimated to be somewhere between 10,000 to 15,000 people.

According to figures from the United Nations, 726,000 Palestinians left Israeli controlled territory between 1947 and 1949. Except for Jordan, Arab refugees who had left Palestine were settled in refugee camps and denied citizenship and civil rights by the Arab countries where they lived.

In the first three years after Israel became a nation, mass immigration doubled the Jewish population. Most of these were Holocaust survivors or Jews fleeing Arab lands.

In 1950, the Knesset passed the law of return, which granted all Jews, those of Jewish ancestry and their spouses, the right to migrate to Israel and become citizens. In the next 20 years, 850,000 Jews left the Arab world to go to Israel.

In 1955, Czechoslovakia began supplying arms to Egypt, while France became Israel's main supplier of arms. The Egyptian government also began recruiting former Nazi rocket scientists to develop a missile program. Tensions grew between Egypt and Israel, and hundreds of Israelis were killed by Fedayeen attacks from Egypt occupied Gaza. Fedayeen attacks led to a growing cycle of violence as Israel launched reprisal attacks against Gaza and the Egyptian government, which organized and sponsored the Fedayeen.

In 1956, Egypt blockaded the Gulf of Aqaba and closed the Suez Canal to Israeli shipping. They then nationalized the canal, which was owned by British and French shareholders. In response to this, France and Britain entered into a secret agreement with Israel to take back the canal by force.

In October 1956, Israeli forces invaded the Gaza Strip and the Sinai, and then pushed on to the Suez Canal. At that time French and British forces stepped in on the pretext of restoring order. They won a quick victory, but had to withdraw from Egypt because of pressure from the United States and the USSR. The United Nations then established a buffer zone with the UN emergency force to keep peace in the area. In return for a withdrawal, Israel was guaranteed freedom of access to the Red Sea and the Suez Canal. In practice, the Suez Canal remained closed to Israeli shipping.

EVALUATION

In this chapter, we have talked about Progressives, Socialists, Communists and Nazis, Fascists, Baron Rothschild, and the banking elite. We haven't mentioned Satan once, and yet he was involved in all of the activities of those just listed.

We haven't mentioned God in this chapter either, but He was also involved in all of these things. The struggle between God and Satan, good and evil, has not ceased. Indeed, the struggle seems to be speeding ever faster toward its climactic end.

Satan doesn't work openly. In fact, he would prefer that you don't even believe that he exists. Nevertheless, he has continued to work furiously behind the scenes. He works by lies and deception through those who do not know the Lord Jesus. He works through the greed of the bankers and the lust for power of the Progressives, Communists and Socialists. He took great delight in Hitler's hatred for the Jews and their slaughter in the Holocaust. In spite of all of this, things do not go smoothly in Satan's kingdom.

Satan's kingdom is made up of people who are motivated by lust, greed, jealousy, anger, hatred, revenge, and lust for power. Therefore, it is not too surprising, to find that Progressives, Socialists and Communists do not always work too well together. That is what is behind all wars. But you can be sure that Satan revels in all the mayhem, blood, and destruction.

God's kingdom is a kingdom of light, justice, peace, and joy. Those of us who have accepted Jesus as our Lord and Savior are a part of His kingdom and will reign with Him. **The victory is ours!**

CHAPTER 14

THE TWENTIETH CENTURY (1961-1980)

JOHN F. KENNEDY (JFK)

In 1960, John F. Kennedy was elected to be the 35th President of the United States. A great many things happened during his short presidency, which was cut short by assassination in 1963. Some people think he was the greatest president who ever lived. Others fault him for his lack of morality and for some very serious mistakes. Almost everyone would have to agree though that he had about him an air of nobility, and his speeches inspired people to think and do great things.

He said, "Ask not what your country can do for you, but what you can do for your country." He had a vision for the Peace Corps and inspired many young men and women to help third world countries become more prosperous. He inspired people with a vision of space travel. He also supported integration and civil rights for minorities. One thing he did though at the beginning of his presidency, would haunt him for the rest of his life.

Before Kennedy's election, President Eisenhower had created a plan to overthrow the Castro government in Cuba. The CIA trained Cubans who had fled Cuba after Castro took power. They would invade Cuba and instigate an uprising among the Cuban people, in hopes of removing Castro from power.

THE CUBAN REVOLUTION

Once again America began interfering in the affairs of another nation to our own hurt and wrecked disaster on the other country. The country was Cuba. Since 1902 Cuba had a republican form of government. During most of the period from the 1930's to the 1950's, a dictator, Fulgencio Batista y Zaldivar, controlled Cuba. On July 26, 1953, Fidel Castro, a young lawyer, tried to start a revolution against Batista at that time he failed but in 1956 he tried again but most of the rebels were either imprisoned or killed. However, Castro and about a dozen of his followers escaped to the Sierra Maestra.

In 1957, Castro's forces began to wage a guerrilla war against the Cuban government. Continued poor economic conditions led to growing support for the rebels. By the middle of 1958, Batista's government had lost the support and confidence of both the United States and the Cubans. In 1959 Fidel Castro was finally successful

Castro's success was aided by The U.S. Government State Department and by the news media. They called him an agrarian reformer. It had been said that Castro was a communist but our government and media downplayed that, but as soon he took over the government his true colors became evident.

The rebels later set up a Communist government, with Castro as its head. The new Cuban government immediately set out to change their status with the United States. In 1960 they seized U.S.-owned businesses, including sugar estates. As a result, relations between Cuba and the United States quickly became strained. Cuba began developing stronger ties with the Soviet Union and in early 1960 they signed an economic pact with the Soviet Union.

On April 17, 1961, only two months after Pres. Kennedy had been sworn in, he ordered the planned invasion of Cuba to proceed. It is known as the Bay of Pigs Invasion. With support from the CIA, 1500 U.S. trained Cuban exiles return to the island with the hope of deposing Castro, but it was doomed to failure.

Unfortunately, the invasion was ordered without US air support or naval support. When the invasion force reached the Bay of Pigs, the Cuban forces turned their artillery on them. Without air and naval support, they didn't have a chance. Pres. Kennedy had not been in on the initial planning; and apparently the CIA, the State Department and the military were not properly coordinated. Of course it is also possible that Kennedy acted on bad advice from Communists in the State Department. In any case, it was a disaster. Many of the invading exiles were killed, and Kennedy was forced to negotiate for the release of 1189 survivors.

CUBAN MISSILE CRISIS

On April 14, 1962, CIA, U-2 spy planes took photographs of Soviet missiles sites under construction in Cuba. This was unacceptable. If nothing was done about it, the Soviets would be able to launch nuclear missiles against the United States at close range. Pres. Kennedy ordered a quarantine of all ships going to Cuba, and gave Khrushchev an ultimatum. Pres. Kennedy and Khrushchev met together a week later. Khrushchev agreed to remove the missiles subject to U.N. inspections if the U.S. publicly promised never to invade Cuba. This was done, and war was averted.

VIETNAM

In Southeast Asia, Kennedy followed Eisenhower's lead by using limited military action as early as 1961 to fight the Communist forces led by Ho Chi Minh. He sent economic and military support to the South Vietnamese government, including 16,000 military advisers and US Special Forces. Kennedy also sanctioned the overthrow of President Diem of South Vietnam, because he was not considered to be anti-Communist enough.

During his time in office, Kennedy increased the number of U.S. military in Vietnam from 800 to 16,300. Those who were close to Pres. Kennedy said that he was strongly considering pulling out of Vietnam before the 1964 election. That never happened, because he was assassinated.

Soon enough, this venture into Vietnam would be shown to be a horrible mistake.

ASSASSINATION

On November 22, 1963, Pres. Kennedy and his wife were on a political trip to Dallas, Texas. As his motorcade just past the Texas School Book Depository and was approaching a grassy knoll shots rang out. Kennedy was shot once in the upper back with a final shot to the head. He was pronounced dead at the hospital about a half an hour later.

The man named as his killer was Lee Harvey Oswald. Oswald claimed that he did not kill anyone, but was set up to be a patsy. He was arrested; but before he could be brought to trial, he was killed by Jack Ruby.

It is my theory that he fired a gun from a window at The School Book Depository, in order to distract attention from the real killers at the grassy knoll. I don't think there's any doubt that he was in on the killing, but I do believe that he was set up to be a patsy. He was then subsequently killed to keep him from telling who the real conspirators were. Similarly, Booth was also killed before trial, to keep him from revealing who wanted Lincoln assassinated.

The bigger question though is who wanted Kennedy killed and why. Shortly before his assassination, Kennedy had made a speech in which he said that he would defend the United States against all enemies both foreign and domestic. He then ordered money printed which bore the Treasury seal, instead of the Federal Reserve seal. The money that he printed was not borrowed and paid no interest to the banks. In my opinion the bankers were not about to tolerate this, so they had him killed. Whether Lyndon Johnson was in on the assassination is an open question in my mind. However, the first thing he did when he became president was to rescind the order to print money. The money that had been printed was kept out of circulation.

PRESIDENT LYNDON B. JOHNSON (LBJ)

John F. Kennedy had asked Johnson to be his running mate for the 1960 presidential election. Following the assassination of Pres. Kennedy, Johnson was sworn into office on Air Force One before leaving for Washington. Now he was president.

He was described by friends, fellow politicians, and historians as motivated throughout his life by an exceptional lust for power and control. As Johnson's biographer, Robert Caro, observes, "Johnson's ambition was uncommon—in the degree to which it was unencumbered by even the slightest excess weight of ideology, of philosophy, of principles, of beliefs."

Pres. Johnson continued many of the programs which had been laid out by Pres. Kennedy. Civil rights was one of those. He signed the Civil Rights Act of 1964, which outlawed most forms of racial segregation. And the 1965, he achieved the passage of a second civil rights bill called the Voting Rights Act, which outlawed discrimination in voting, thus allowing millions of Southern blacks to vote for the first time.

Pres. Johnson also continued JFK's space program. Right before Johnson left office in December 1968, the Apollo 8 space vehicle made a successful flight to the moon and back.

Pres. Johnson, not only continued JFK's foray into Vietnam, but also greatly expanded it. At Kennedy's death, there were 16,000 American military advisers in Vietnam. Johnson escalated the war continuously from 1964 to 1968. By 1968 there were over 550,000 American soldiers inside Vietnam, and they were being killed at the rate of over 1000 month.

Johnson tried to fight the war with three strikes against him.

Strike number one: He tried to pursue the war, while at the same time trying to realize his ideas of the Great Society. Early on in his presidency he made a speech in which he proclaimed to the American people that we could have "both guns and butter."

Strike number two: He tried to fight the war with a policy of containment. He tried very hard to win, but he was afraid to do the things necessary to win. He was afraid that China and Russia would enter the war. It was a policy doomed to failure.

Strike number three: As casualties mounted, Johnson's popularity plummeted. College students and others protested, burned draft cards and chanted, "Hey, hey LBJ, how many kids did you kill today?"

Pres. Johnson realized that his base of support had eroded. Therefore, at the end of the speech he gave March 31, 1968, he announced, "I shall not seek, nor will I accept the nomination of my party for another term as your president."

OTHER NOTABLE EVENTS DURING THE JOHNSON ADMINISTRATION

1. **"War on poverty"** In 1964, Johnson set in motion bills and acts which created programs such as head start, food stamps, Medicare and Medicaid.
2. **Major riots** took place in black neighborhoods in different places. There were riots in Harlem in 1964 and in the Watts district of Los Angeles in 1965. Six days of rioting in Newark left 26 dead and 1500 injured. Things were so bad in Detroit, in 1967 that Gov. Romney sent 7400 National Guard troops to stop the fire bombing, looting, and attack upon business and the police. Finally, Pres. Johnson sent in federal troops with tanks and machine guns. Detroit continued to riot for three more days until 43 people were dead, 2250 were injured, 4000 were arrested and property damage ran into hundreds of millions of dollars.
3. **Dr. Martin Luther King** was assassinated April 4, 1968 in Memphis, Tennessee. Riots then occurred in over 100 cities.
4. **The Six-Day War:** The Arab world had decided to push the Israelis into the Mediterranean

Sea. In May of 1967, president Nasser of Egypt expelled United Nations forces that stood as a buffer between Egypt and Israel. Egypt then moved 1000 tanks and nearly 100,000 soldiers to the Israeli border, and closed the Straits of Tiran to all ships flying the Israeli flag. On May 30, Jordan and Egypt signed a defense pact and the Iraqi army began to deploy troops and armored units in Jordan. On June 5, 1967, Israel launched a preemptive air attack against Egypt. They caught the Egyptian planes on the ground and destroyed them. The war lasted six days. Israel conquered the Sinai Peninsula, Jerusalem, and the West Bank. Israel vowed at that time that they would never again give up Jerusalem.

RICHARD M. NIXON

In 1968, Richard Nixon won the election to become the 37th president of the United States. Nixon inherited the Vietnam War. He had promised during the campaign to get America out of Vietnam. When Nixon took office, 300 American soldiers were dying per week. He first approved a secret bombing campaign of North Vietnamese positions in Cambodia. He then proposed simultaneous withdrawals of North Vietnamese and of American forces from Vietnam. In June 1969, he reduced troop strength by 25,000 American soldiers. The idea was to replace American troops with Vietnamese troops. American involvement in the war continued to decline until a complete pull out was made in 1973. Peace accords were finally signed in 1973. At this point the North Vietnamese troops were gone and the South Vietnamese were supposed to be able to defend their own borders. North Vietnam had other ideas. As soon as all the American troops had departed the North Vietnamese troops returned. In 1975, without American support, South Vietnam fell to the North.

The Vietnam War was a disaster. About 58,000 Americans died in the war. South Vietnamese deaths exceeded a million, and North Vietnam lost between 500,000 and 1 million troops. The effect of the war on the American psychological and moral foundations was even more devastating than the numbers of those killed. For the first time in history America had lost a war, a war that could have been won. Most Americans no longer wanted anything to do with the military. America's parents were no longer willing to see their children go off to die. America was no longer willing to tolerate American losses in any future war.

From the moral standpoint, the rebellion, which began on the college campuses against the war, extended to sex and every other area of the social fabric of society. The effects of the Vietnam War will still be felt a hundred years from now should this world survive so long.

Nixon came to the presidency with lofty ambitions. He wanted to develop peaceful relationships with America's enemies. He also wanted to help bring peace to the Middle East, to restrain inflation, and reform welfare.

In 1972, he visited China, and opened diplomatic relations between the United States and China. He then initiated the Anti-Ballistic Missile Treaty with the Soviet Union. His foreign policy initiatives were largely successful, but he didn't do so well on the domestic front.

By the time Nixon assumed the office of president, inflation was already on the rise. Many years of the Vietnamese war, along with Pres. Johnson's "guns and butter" spending meant that the country was going ever deeper into debt. Whenever money is spent that is created out of thin air, inflation always results

For a short time Nixon tried to combat inflation by a wage and price freeze. He was pretty successful freezing wages, but not prices. He soon gave up on that idea, but then ran into another economic problem.

President Franklin Roosevelt had set the price of gold at \$35 per ounce. While the people in the United States were not able to own or trade in gold, it was still used in international trade. People from other countries were able to purchase gold at \$35 an ounce. Because the United States had been running the printing press and inflation had taken hold, they knew the dollar was losing value. Therefore; they began to take advantage of being able to buy gold for \$35 an ounce. By the time Nixon took office, US gold reserves had declined from \$25 billion to \$10.5 billion. Nixon rightly thought that if this continued, pretty soon the United States would not have any more gold.

Nixon's solution to the problem was to announce to the world that the United States would no longer honor their commitment to sell gold for \$35 an ounce. From now on, the price of gold would be whatever the market would bear. When countries objected to the new policy, Nixon said, "That's your problem." Indeed it was their problem. The United States economy was the largest in the world and the US dollar had for a long time been the reserve currency of the world. If other countries wanted to continue to trade with the United States they had no choice but to continue to use the US Dollar.

The dollar was now like a ship drifting in the sea without an anchor or a rudder. From now on, inflation of the dollar would accelerate.

It was during the Nixon presidency, that the Supreme Court issued its Roe vs. Wade ruling legalizing abortion. This began the process whereby about 55 million babies have been slaughtered.

In 1969, during Nixon's first year in office, the United States sent three men to the moon, becoming the first nation until now to do so.

Tensions had been growing along the border of the Soviet Union and China. Nixon decided to use their conflict to shift the balance of power toward the West.

He reduced trade restrictions with China and sent covert messages to them of friendship. After receiving an invitation from Chou En-lai, Nixon visited China. That visit has changed our relationship with China ever since.

Next, Nixon met with the Soviet leader Leonid Brezhnev. The two of them proclaimed a new era of "peaceful coexistence."

At this time, Nixon was a very popular president. His foreign policy initiatives were considered a great success, and his domestic policies were considered at least average or above. When it came time for the 1972 election, he was re-nominated and ran against George McGovern, the Democratic standard bearer. Nixon was reelected with one of the largest landslide election victories in history. He defeated George McGovern, with over 60% of the popular vote, losing only the state of Massachusetts and the District of Columbia.

On October 10, 1973, Vice President Agnew resigned because of charges of bribery, tax evasion, and money laundering while he was governor of Maryland. Nixon chose Gerald Ford, the Republican minority leader in the House of Representatives, to replace him.

In October 1973, an Arab coalition led by Egypt and Syria attacked Israel in what is known as the Yom Kippur War. To begin with, Israel suffered losses and appealed to European countries for help. The Europeans did nothing to help except for the Netherlands, but Pres. Nixon sent an airlift of American arms to Israel.

American help to Israel came with a price. Members of OPEC, oil exporting countries, decided to raise the price and cut production of oil, in retaliation for America's help to Israel.

The OPEC nations were already unhappy with United States, because Nixon chose to go off the gold standard. After doing this, the price of gold went up, but the value of the dollar declined. Since oil was paid for in dollars, OPEC was receiving less value for their product. They cut production and announced price hikes as well as an embargo against the United States and the Netherlands, who also helped Israel. In January 1974, Nixon signed a bill that limited the speed limit to 55 mph, in order to save gas during the crisis.

WATERGATE

Democratic Party headquarters was located at the Watergate Hotel in Washington DC. Five men were caught breaking in and bugging the Democratic headquarters. They were linked to a committee for reelecting the president. They were trying to find out what the Democrats were planning.

Nixon claimed that he didn't know anything about it until afterwards. That is probably true, but Nixon did try to help his aides cover it up. Nixon had a secret taping system that recorded conversations and phone calls in the Oval Office. This would prove to be his undoing. The Nixon's tapes were subpoenaed. The tapes did not prove that he was guilty of anything other than a cover-up to help his aides. Nevertheless, he had lost political support and faced the near certainty of impeachment hearings.

On August 8, 1974 he went on the radio and gave a speech in which he announced his resignation and that Vice President Gerald Ford would take over as president, effective at noon Eastern Time, the next day.

On September 8, 1974, Pres. Ford granted Nixon a "full, free, and absolute pardon." This ended any possibility of an indictment against Nixon. After this, Nixon released a statement:

> I was wrong in not acting more decisively and forthrightly in dealing with Watergate.... No words can describe the depths of my regret and pain at the anguish of my mistakes over Watergate have caused the nation and presidency, a nation I so deeply love and an institution I so greatly respect

Even though Pres. Nixon left his office in disgrace, he was later recognized as an elder statesman and was ranked by gallop poll as one of the 10 most admired men in the world.

PRES. GERALD FORD
Within a month after Pres. Ford pardoned Nixon, his approval rating dropped from 71% to 49%. Pres. Ford was troubled

by inflation, but was ineffective in being able to do anything about it.

One of Ford's greatest challenges was dealing with the continued conflict in Vietnam. After the Paris peace accords had been signed, America had no more direct involvement in Vietnam. The peace accords, however, called for the territorial integrity of Vietnam, and for national elections to be held in both the North and the South.

In a number of letters to the South Vietnamese president, Nixon had promised that the United States would defend his government, should the North Vietnamese violate the accords.

In December 1974, just months after Ford took office; North Vietnamese forces invaded the South. As North Vietnamese forces advanced, Ford requested a $522 million dollar aid package, but the Democratic Congress refused, even though these funds had been promised by the Nixon administration. President Thieu of South Vietnam resigned and publicly blamed the lack of support from the United States for the fall of his country.

PRESIDENT JIMMY CARTER (1977-1981)

In 1976, Jimmy Carter won the election over Gerald Ford. Many people still held Ford's pardon of Nixon against him. Jimmy Carter on the other hand, seemed to be a sincere, honest, and well meaning Southerner.

On his first day in office, he pardoned all those who dodged the draft during Vietnam War. However, he did not pardoned deserters.

One of the highlights of his presidency was his inviting the Egyptian President Anwar Sadat and Israeli Prime Minister Begin for talks at Camp David. This led to a formal peace treaty in 1979. In addition, diplomatic relations were formally established between China and the United States in 1979. Also, throughout his career, he emphasized human rights.

His whole time in office was plagued by stagflation. Stagflation really wasn't his fault, but he didn't know what to do about it. Stagflation is a combination of inflation plus recession.

Whenever banks print money, the result is always inflation. During the Vietnam War, the Federal Reserve printed lots of money to loan to the government. By the time Richard Nixon became president, inflation was well on its way. When he closed the gold window inflation accelerated and by the time Carter became president, the economy had already begun to slow down.

Ordinarily, Keynesian economists would have recommended spending more money in order to stimulate the economy. The problem is that if you spend more borrowed money, it adds to the inflation, which is part of the problem. If you taxed more in order to spend more, you would be taking more money out of private hands. If you did that, people would have less money to spend, businesses would have less money to invest, and it would slow the economy even more. Keynesians didn't have the answer, and Carter didn't know what to do. It would take the next president, Ronald Reagan, to solve the problem.

The final year of Carter's presidency was marred by lots of trouble. First of all, there was a near meltdown of the nuclear core at the Three Mile Island nuclear generating station. On March 28, 1979, the valves stuck open, which allowed a large amount of the reactor coolant to escape. Finally, they were able to get more water in and shut the reactor down. No one was killed or injured, but the accident shocked the nation, and no new nuclear plants have been built.

In Iran there was a revolution. The Shah of Iran resigned and the Islamists seized the government. On November 4, 1969, students seized the US embassy in Teheran and 60 Americans were taken hostage. They soon allow the women to leave, but 52 hostages were held for more than a year.

Pres. Carter responded by imposing economic sanctions on Iran. He then sent a small military force to try and rescue the hostages, but three of the helicopters malfunctioned. They were unable to continue the rescue operation. Eventually, the volatile Khomeini agreed to release the hostages in exchange for unfreezing Iranian assets. However, they were not released until Reagan became president.

During the presidency of Jimmy Carter, the misery index reached its highest level in history. The unemployment rate plus the inflation rate equals the misery index.

During the presidential campaign of 1976, Jimmy Carter also made mention of the misery index, which at that time stood at 13.57. When he ran for president again in 1980 against Ronald Reagan, the misery index had reached 21.98%, the highest in history. Reagan won.

CHAPTER 15

THE TWENTIETH CENTURY (1981-2000)

PRESIDENT RONALD REAGAN

Ronald Reagan was born in Tampico, Illinois, February 6, 1911. He first began his career in radio. In 1937 he moved to California and appeared in 52 movies. Reagan served as the president of the Screen Actors Guild. Later he moved into television and was the star of the General Electric Theater.

Originally he was a Democrat, but he switched to the Republican Party in 1962. As he explained it, he did not leave the Democratic Party, the Democratic Party left him. When Barry Goldwater was running for president in 1964, Reagan delivered a very powerful and rousing speech in support of Barry Goldwater. Goldwater lost the election, but many people saw Reagan's political talent. He was persuaded to run for governor of California, which he did and won two years later, in 1966, and again in 1970.

In the 1980 presidential campaign, Ronald Reagan ran against Jimmy Carter. He promised to bring the hostages back from Iran. He also called attention to the misery index that Carter often referred to when he ran against Pres. Ford.

Reagan asked, "Are you better off now than you were four years ago?" Reagan also stressed lowering taxes to stimulate the economy, less government interference in people's lives, states rights, and a strong national defense. Reagan won the election, carrying 44 states with 489 electoral votes to 49 electoral votes for Carter. At 69, Ronald Reagan was the oldest man ever elected to the office of the presidency.

In his first inaugural address on January 20, 1981, Reagan stated, "In this present crisis, government is not the solution to our problems; government is the problem."

While he was yet giving the inaugural address, Iran released 52 US hostages, which they had held for 444 days.

About two months later, on March 30, 1981, Reagan, his Press Secretary James Brady, and two others were shot by a would-be assassin, John Hinckley Jr. The bullet struck Reagan's lung and came within an inch of his heart. His condition was very serious, but he survived and quickly recovered. James Brady was not so fortunate. He survived but was paralyzed from the waist down. Reagan believed that God had spared his life so that he might go on to fulfill a greater purpose.

Only a few months later in August 1981, the federal traffic controllers went on strike. This was a violation of a regulation which prohibited government unions from striking. Reagan held a press conference and stated that if the air traffic controllers did not go back to work within 48 hours, they would be fired.

Many of the traffic controllers did not believe that Reagan would go through with his threat, but Reagan proved to be a man of his word. On August 5, 1981, he fired 11,345 striking air traffic controllers.

THE ECONOMY

During Jimmy Carter's last year in office, inflation averaged 12.5 compared to 4.4% during Reagan's last year in office. Over the next three years, the unemployment rate also declined from 7.5% to 5.3%.

Reagan's policies were based on supply-side economics. He believed that businesses should be free from overregulation, and that they should be allowed to do what they do best. He sought to stimulate the economy through large across-the-board tax cuts.

His critics claimed that Reagan's tax cuts would create great deficits and increase the national debt. Reagan, on the other hand, claimed that the reduction in taxes would actually stimulate the economy to such an extent that even more taxes would be collected. He was right.

During Reagan's presidency, federal income taxes were lowered significantly. The top tax rate went from 70% to 28%. Yet, federal income tax receipts almost doubled from 1980 to 1989. Ironically, the deficit also went up slightly. This was because Congress insisted on spending every dime that came in, plus some. Reagan tried everything he could to get Congress to cut spending, but they wouldn't go along.

LEBANON

America had a military presence in Lebanon as part of a multinational peacekeeping force during the Lebanese civil war. On October 23, 1983, a suicide truck bomber destroyed the American barracks in Beirut, Lebanon, which resulted in the deaths of 241 servicemen with 60 others wounded.

Reagan called the attack, 'despicable' and pledged to keep a military force in Lebanon. He planned to target the Sheik Abdullah barracks, which was a training ground for Hezbollah fighters. The mission, however, was aborted, and he instead ordered the Marines to begin withdrawing from Lebanon.

THE COLD WAR GETS COLDER

Reagan ordered a buildup of the United States military. He revived the B-1 bomber project and the MX peacekeeper missile that Carter had canceled. Also, in response to Soviet deployment of the SS-20 missile, he oversaw NATO's deployment of the Pershing II missile in West Germany. Reagan believed that the only way to achieve peace was through strength.

Under a policy that became known as the Reagan doctrine, his administration provided aid to anti-communist movements all over the world.

In March of 1983, Reagan introduced the Strategic Defense Initiative (SDI), a defense project that would use ground and space-based systems to protect the United States from attack by strategic nuclear ballistic missiles. The Soviets became concerned about this and said that SDI would put the whole world in jeopardy.

Critics labeled Reagan's foreign policy as aggressive, imperialistic, and warmongering. However, it cannot be disputed that Reagan's policies kept us out of any kind of major wars, and actually ended the Cold War.

REAGAN'S SECOND TERM
In 1984, Reagan was elected for the second time, winning 49 states

Relations with Libya suddenly went from bad to worse. In April 1986, a bomb exploded at a Berlin disco tech, resulting in the injury of 63 American military personnel and the death of one serviceman. After Reagan received irrefutable proof that Libya had directed the terrorist bombing, Reagan ordered the use of force against the country. On the evening of April 15, 1996, the US launched a series of airstrikes on ground targets in Libya. The president addressed the nation from the Oval Office after the attacks and said, "When our citizens are attacked or abused anywhere in the world on the direct orders of hostile regimes, we will respond so long as I am in this office."

IMMIGRATION REFORM
In 1986, Reagan signed the immigration Reform and Control Act. This act made it illegal to knowingly hire or recruit illegal aliens. It required employers to attest to their employee's immigration status. This was supposed to stop illegal immigration. This bill also granted amnesty to 3 million illegal immigrants who had entered the United States prior to January 1, 1982. Unfortunately, Congress refused to do what was necessary to stop the illegal immigration.

IRAN-CONTRA
In 1986, a scandal shook the administration stemming from the use of proceeds from covert arms sales to Iran to fund the Contras in Nicaragua. Democrats in Congress didn't like the

way Reagan was fighting against the Communists. Therefore they passed a law specifically forbidding aid to the Contras in Nicaragua.

Pres. Reagan said that he didn't know anything about this and appointed two Republicans and one Democrat, to investigate. The commission could not find direct evidence that Reagan had any prior knowledge of the program, but criticized him for not managing his staff better. The scandal resulted in 14 members of Reagan's staff being indicted with 11 of them being convicted.

THE END OF THE COLD WAR

After World War II the United States had allowed the military to deteriorate, while the USSR had built up their military arsenal. Pres. Reagan began to correct the situation. The Soviets were not able to keep up with America's military buildup because of their inefficient economy. At the same time, Reagan persuaded Saudi Arabia to increase its oil production, which resulted in a drop of oil prices. Since Soviet revenues were based on the export of oil, their economy slowed down.

After Mikhail Gorbachev became the new Soviet leader, Reagan recognized a change in the direction of leadership and decided to use diplomacy to try to encourage the Soviet leader to pursue substantial arms agreements. Reagan's personal mission was to free the world of nuclear weapons.

Speaking at the Berlin wall on June 12, 1987 Reagan gave Gorbachev a challenge, he said:

"General Secretary Gorbachev, if you seek peace, if you seek prosperity for the Soviet Union and Eastern Europe, if you seek liberalization, come here to this gate! Mr.

Gorbachev, open this gate! Mr. Gorbachev, tear down this wall".

At Reagan's third meeting with Gorbachev in 1987, they signed The Intermediate Range Nuclear Forces Treaty at the White House. This treaty eliminated an entire class of nuclear weapons. They also laid the framework for the Strategic Arms Reduction Treaty. In 1989, the Berlin Wall was torn down. Two years later the Soviet Union collapsed.

PRESIDENT GEORGE H. W. BUSH (1989-1993)
He was Ronald Reagan's vice president, a former naval aviator during World War II, a congressman, an ambassador, a director of central intelligence, and a member of the "Skull and Bones" while he was at Yale University.

In 1988, Bush won the Republican nomination for president, and went on to win the election over Michael Dukakis. At the Republican national convention, Bush had given what was known as his "thousand points of light speech". In this speech, he described his vision for America. He endorsed the prayer of allegiance, prayer in schools, capital punishment, gun rights, and he opposed abortion. He made one more comment in that speech that he should not have made unless he intended to keep it. He said. "Read my lips: no new taxes". That statement would come back to haunt him and caused him to lose his bid for reelection.

Early in his term, Bush faced the problem of deficits that had grown larger during the Reagan administration. Bush pressed the Democratic controlled Congress to do something about the deficit. The Republicans in Congress said the best way to cut the deficit is to cut spending. But the Democrats insisted that the only way would be to raise taxes. Bush eventually surrendered to the Democrats and raised taxes. This alienated him from conservative Republicans and cost him the next election.

When Bush ran against Reagan for the presidential nomination in 1980, he had referred to Reagan's ideas concerning the economy as "Voodoo Economics". Now he was about to receive an economics lesson. A mild recession ensued, which was followed by an increasing unemployment rate. This caused an increase in many government welfare programs. Many Republicans and Independents who had supported him were very unhappy.

In July 1991, Bush and Gorbachev signed the Strategic Arms Reduction Treaty. The Treaty would reduce the US and USSR's strategic nuclear weapons by about 35% over seven years, and the Soviet Union's land-based intercontinental ballistic missiles would be cut by 50%.

PERSIAN GULF WAR

On August 1, 1990, Saddam Hussein of Iraq, invaded Kuwait, his oil-rich neighbor. Bush condemned the invasion and began rallying opposition to Iraq with world leaders. King Fahd of Saudi Arabia requested US military aid, because he was afraid Iraq would also invade his country.

Hussein tried to make a deal that would allow his country to take control of half of Kuwait. Bush rejected this deal and insisted instead on a complete withdrawal of all Iraqi forces from Kuwait, and that Kuwait's legitimate government must be restored.

In a speech to the United States Congress, Bush said that, "the security and stability of the Persian Gulf must be

assured. And American citizens abroad must be protected."
He then outlined a fifth, long-term objective:

> "Out of these troubled times, our fifth objective — a
> new world order — can emerge: a new era — freer from
> the threat of terror, stronger in the pursuit of justice, and
> more secure in the quest for peace. An era in which the
> nations of the world, East and West, North and South,
> can prosper and live in harmony....A world, where the
> rule of law supplants the rule of the jungle.
>
> A world, in which nations recognize the shared
> responsibility for freedom and justice. A world where the
> strong respect the rights of the weak"

The illuminati and its organizations had long advocated
for a New World Order. The book of Revelation in the Bible
had prophesied about a New World Order, but this was the
first time a United States leader actually talked about it.

INVASION OF IRAQ

The U.S. Congress approved the invasion of Iraq. Early in
the morning of January 17, 1991, Allied forces launched the
first attack of more than 4000 bombing runs. This continued
until a ground invasion February 24th pushed toward Kuwait
City and Iraqi forces fled, retreating toward Bagdad. President
Bush stopped the offensive after only 100 hours to save lives.
Bush's approval rating went up after the successful offensive,
but did come down somewhat after people began to criticize
him for not overthrowing the Iraqi government. Bush did not
want to overthrow the Iraqi government, because that would
have meant he would've had to occupy Baghdad, and in effect
rule Iraq.

At the end of this conflict, Bush and Gorbachev agreed that the world had now begun a New World Order.

In 1992, Bush again ran for president. He was opposed by the Democrat Bill Clinton and a third party candidate Ross Perot. Ross Perot claimed that neither Republicans nor Democrats could fix America's economic problems. He received more votes than any other third party candidate had ever received. But when the votes were counted, Bill Clinton was very decisively elected; mainly because Bush had made a promise of no new taxes which he very foolishly broke. The people never forgot.

PRESIDENT WILLIAM JEFFERSON CLINTON (1996-2001)

In his inaugural address, January 20, 1993, he declared: "Our democracy must be not only the envy of the world, but the engine of our own renewal. There is nothing wrong with America that cannot be cured by what is right with America."

In his first address to the nation on February 15, he stated his intention to raise taxes to fix the budget deficit. One of the next things he did was to attempt to fulfill a campaign promise of allowing homosexual men and women to serve in the Armed Forces. This caused a considerable debate in Congress, and finally resulted into a **"Don't ask, don't tell"** policy. This meant that as long as homosexuals kept their sexuality a secret, they could serve in the military.

Also in 1993, Clinton supported the ratification of the **North American Free Trade Agreement**. This agreement had been negotiated by George Bush but came under a great deal of fire from some Republicans, Democrats and supporters of Ross Perot. With Clinton's support, the bill passed both the House and the Senate; and on January 1, 1994, Clinton signed it into law. This trade agreement was considered a very important first step for America toward a **New World Order.**

One of the most prominent failures of the Clinton agenda, though, was the universal health-care reform plan, which was spearheaded by Hillary Clinton.

In spite of Clinton's party holding a majority in both houses of Congress, the effort to create a national health care system ultimately died.

SCANDALS AND CONTROVERSIES

When Bill Clinton came to the White House, scandal and charges of various kinds of wrong doing came with him. Long before Clinton became president, he had earned his nick name, "Slick Willy".

TRAVELGATE CONTROVERSY

In May 1993, Clinton fires seven employees of the White House Travel Office. The White House claimed the firings were done because of financial improprieties alleged by the FBI. Critics maintain that the firings were done to allow friends of the Clintons to take over the travel office business, and that there was no reason for the FBI to be involved.

WHITEWATER CONTROVERSY

The Whitewater controversy was over a failed business venture in the Whitewater Development Corporation that Bill and Hillary had with Jim and Susan McDougal. In November 1993, David Hale alleged that Clinton while governor of Arkansas, pressured him to provide an illegal loan of $300,000 to Susan McDougal, who was a partner of the Clintons in the Whitewater land deal.

The McDougal's were eventually charged and convicted of wrongdoing, but the Clintons were never charged. Susan McDougal spent a long time in jail for contempt of court, because she would not testify against Bill Clinton.

TROOPERGATE

Two Arkansas State Troopers claimed that they had arranged sexual liaisons for then Gov. Bill Clinton at his request. One of the women named in the allegation was a woman by the name of Paula Jones.

THE WHITE HOUSE FBI FILES CONTROVERSY

In June 1996, a controversy arose because Craig Livingstone, head of the White House Office of Personnel Security, improperly requested, and received from the FBI background reports of individuals who had been employed by the Republican administration.

WOMEN IN BILL'S LIFE

Paula Jones brought a lawsuit against Clinton for sexual harassment, while he was president. However, a US judge in Arkansas, Susan Webber Wright ruled that since Jones had not suffered any damages, the case should be dismissed. This judge had been one of Clinton's students at the University of Arkansas. On April 2, 1998, Judge Wright dismissed the Jones lawsuit. In July, Jones filed an appeal and prevailed. During the deposition, Clinton denied having sexual relations with Monica Lewinsky -- a denial that became the basis for impeachment charges of perjury.

On November 18, 1999, Clinton agreed to an out-of-court settlement of $850,000, however he still offered Jones no apology and denied that he had ever had a sexual affair with her.

In 1998, **Kathleen Willey** charged that Clinton had sexually assaulted her four years previously, and **Juanita Broaddrick** claimed that Clinton raped her. Some 20 years previously.

Other women, who said they had adulterous relations with Bill Clinton, were: **Gennifer Flowers, Elizabeth Gracen, Sally Perdue, and Dolly Browning.**

THE LEWINSKY SCANDAL

In 1998, the House of Representatives voted to impeach President Clinton because he lied about his relationship with Monica Lewinsky in a sworn deposition in the Paula Jones lawsuit. Bill Clinton was charged with perjury and obstruction of justice.

After a 21 day trial, the Senate failed to convict Bill Clinton, on either count. In my opinion the Republican leaders in the Senate had already determined not to convict him before any evidence was presented, therefore the trial was just for show because the Constitution required it.

In 2000, the Arkansas Supreme Court's Committee on Professional Conduct, called for Clinton's disbarment saying that he lied about his affair with Monica Lewinsky. Clinton was fined $25,000, and his Arkansas law license was suspended for five years. Clinton also resigned from the Supreme Court bar, in November.

MILITARY AND FOREIGN EVENTS

Numerous military skirmishes and foreign events occurred during Clinton's presidency.

In 1993, the Battle of Mogadishu in Somalia occurred, in which two Black Hawk helicopters were shot down, after which US forces were withdrawn from Somalia.

In 1995 U.S. and NATO aircraft attacked Bosnian Serb targets to halt attacks on UN safe zones and to pressure them into a peace accord. Later that year, Clinton deployed US peacekeepers to Bosnia

In response to Al Qaeda bombings of US Embassy's in East Africa, Clinton in 1998, ordered cruise missile strikes on terrorist targets in Afghanistan and Sudan. He was later criticized because it turned out that what they thought to be a chemical warfare plant was actually a pharmaceutical plant in Sudan which had now been destroyed.

In 1999, Clinton authorized the use of American troops in a NATO bombing campaign against Yugoslavia in order to stop ethnic cleansing.. Kosovo was eventually placed under UN administration and the president of Yugoslavia Slobodan Milosevic was charged with the murders of about 600 ethnic Albanians and crimes against humanity

In Clinton's 1998 State of the Union address, he warned Congress of Saddam Hussein's possible pursuit of nuclear weapons.

SUMMARY STATEMENT OF THE CLINTON PRESIDENCY

Bill Clinton is without a doubt one of the smartest, shrewdest, most pragmatic man who has ever been elected to be President of the United States.

Clinton came to the White House in a fairly prosperous time, and whenever the economy started to slack, a compliant Alan Greenspan of the Federal Reserve increased the money supply. All recessions were aborted. Aborting recessions does not get rid of the problem, it just delays it, making correction later much more difficult.

In spite of all his immoral behavior and scandals, Clinton remained popular with the people, ending his presidential career with a 63% approval rating. He still remains popular, and if it were possible he would probably be reelected as President tomorrow.

CHAPTER 16

THE 20TH CENTURY — IN RETROSPECT

SATAN'S PLAN -- ALMOST COMPLETE

As the 20th century was coming to a close, Satan must have been absolutely giddy with excitement. His plan was almost complete. He was so close. All that was needed was a little push here or little nudge there. Soon, everything would fall into place. He had been at this place before, when victory seemed assured. But something he had not thought of always robbed him of victory. This time though, he thought to himself: "I will succeed. I have planned out every detail for the last 400 years and I will bring it to pass."

JUST WHAT IS SATAN'S PLAN?

Satan's plan is to establish his kingdom upon this earth. His plan is to steal the hearts, minds and the souls of men. Satan wants to receive the praise, the honor, the worship, and adoration that belong only to God.

HOW WOULD SATAN WORK HIS PLAN?

Satan realized that for his plan to work, he would have to stamp out the knowledge of and the worship of the true God.

But, he thought, how can I do that? In the early history of the Christian Church, he tried to get rid of Christians through persecution and death. The problem was that the blood of the martyrs became the seed of the church.

Then he tried to destroy the church, by bringing in idolatry, by keeping the Bible in a language that the people could not read, and by chaining the Bible to the pulpit. He almost had victory, but then along came Martin Luther.

Satan came to realize that for his plan to work the way he wanted it to, he would have to be in control of all the kingdoms of the world. He would have to be able to control both men's thoughts and their actions. In order to accomplish this, he would need power, lots of power.

POWER TO WORK SATAN'S PLAN

Satan had a problem. How could he project the kind of power that was needed to accomplish his purpose? Under the restraints that God had placed upon him, Satan could not so much as lift a feather. All he could do was whisper thoughts into the minds of those who are willing to listen to him. But that had been enough to do great damage. It had been enough to cause God to send a flood that almost destroyed mankind. Satan had been using this method with individuals, kings, and religious authorities, ever since. However, it was not enough, to accomplish his purposes now. Something else was needed. Satan discovered that the key to power was money.

KEY TO THE POWER OF MONEY – BANKING

The key to power is money, but that kind of power was not available to ordinary money. Gold and silver had been used for money for thousands of years. But there was a problem with gold and silver. It had to be mined. It was heavy, bulky, had to be stored, was difficult to move, and it could be easily stolen. No, for the kind of power that Satan needed, this would not do. Satan needed the ability to create his own money out of nothing. He needed the power of Fractional Reserve Banking.

In the 17th and 18th centuries, modern banking began to develop. About the middle of the 18th century, Satan found a man by the name of Mayer Amschel Rothschild. He would use this man and his family to project his power. Today, the Rothschild extended family either owns, controls, or influences almost every bank in the world.

HOW HAS SATAN USED THE POWER OF MONEY THROUGH HIS SURROGATES TO ADVANCE HIS KINGDOM?

1. He has pitted countries and kingdoms against each other. He has used greed, envy, distrust, and a lust for power to keep nations at each other's throats. He used his surrogates to loan money for countries to buy weapons of war, so they could defend their borders. Then he would instigate wars to see the blood flow. No ruler would dare try defrauding any of his banks either because they knew he had banks all over the world, and he could lend money to their enemies.

2. He has used money to buy influence. He provided money for Adam Weishaupt in the 1770s to write out the master plan of Satan, and to organize the Illuminati, who would

carry out the plan. He provided money to universities, which would hire the Professors to speak for him. He provided the money for Charles Darwin to write and publish his book called, "The Origin of the Species." He provided money and support for Karl Marx to be able to write and publish "The Communist Manifesto" on February 21, 1848.

Through the centuries, Satan has used money to influence Kings and rulers. In America, he has used money to finance the election campaigns of those he wants in power as well as to bribe officials already elected to office.

HOW HAS SATAN ADVANCED HIS KINGDOM DURING THE 20TH CENTURY?

At the beginning of the 20th century, Satan started using Progressives and progressive thought to accomplish his agenda. The Progressives were reformers who couldn't be bothered with old-fashioned things such as the Bible, the Constitution of the United States, the thinking of our founding fathers, or the Bill of Rights. Satan used the Progressives to start many important parts of his agenda. Such as:

1. **The Federal Reserve Bank.** This was absolutely essential so that Satan would have the money he needed to undermine the United States and establish his kingdom.

2. **Progressive Education.** It was necessary to dumb down the American people beginning with the children so that they would not know or understand their heritage. History would

have to be rewritten. The founding fathers would have to be smeared and the Constitution declared insufficient for today's society.

3. **Control of the media.** He had his people buy up all the major newspapers and radio and TV networks.

4. **The League of Nations.** It was important to start getting the nations together so that he could influence all nations at the same time, and prepare the way for a One World Government under his control.

5. **Council of Foreign Relations (CFR).** The purpose of the CFR was to get important leaders of government, business, banks, and the media together to secretly set policy and work toward certain goals. The media especially needed to be involved in this so that news stories could be spun in the right way.

6. **Expertise in Propaganda.** Under Woodrow Wilson, propaganda was developed into a fine art. It was so good in fact, that later the Nazis copied it for their propaganda machine.

7. **Break down of Morality.** In 1920, Satan used Margaret Sanger to publish a book called "Breeding the Thoroughbred." In this book, she called for unrestrained sexuality, abortion, and sterilization. She wanted to breed a master race. In order to accomplish this, she wanted to sterilize blacks, Jews, southern Europeans, fundamentalist Christians, and the mentally impaired. She was also the founder of Planned

Parenthood. She was heavily funded by the Rockefeller and Ford foundations.

8. **Establishment of a Communist Regime in Russia.** This was important to establish a state of tension and crisis in the world. Satan is able to use tension and crisis to create fear, cause governments to arm themselves, borrow money, pass all kinds of laws and regulations that Satan would now be able to use for his own purposes.

9. **Infiltrate universities and seminaries.** Satan was able by the enticement of status and prestige to get professors to go to Europe to study. In this way, he was able to get destructive European thought, philosophies, and liberal theology brought to the United States. The purpose was to undermine the church, American society, and make many people forget what made America great.

In the meantime, millions of Russian peasants were starving to death, because of the policies of their communist rulers. Satan was delighted.

All of this Satan was able to accomplish during the first 20 years of the 20th century. For the rest of the 20th century, Satan would continue doing the things that he had started. He knew that it would take several generations for the things he had started to take full effect. Before he could take over the world, these programs would have to run their course.

During the 1920s, many people began to see that some of the things the Progressives were doing were not good.

Progressivism began to get a bad name. So Progressives began to call themselves liberals.

By the way, progressive liberal thought has infiltrated both political parties. From 1932 on, all Presidents of either political party were approved by the Council of Foreign Relations except for Ronald Reagan. The Council of Foreign Relations approves both the Republican and Democratic candidates so that no matter who wins the election, their agenda will be advanced.

During the following decades, Satan took great delight in the suffering brought about by the Great Depression and the wars that followed it. However, his main objective was to capture the hearts, minds, and souls of men.

By the end of the 20th century, Satan must have been quite happy with himself. The combination of liberal theology and progressive education had so weakened the churches that many people quit going to church. America had gradually begun to lose its status as a Christian nation.

Satan had used progressive education for several generations now, to keep children ignorant of both their political, cultural, and religious heritage. Now, a whole generation had grown up which was ignorant of their heritage. They were now ready for a takeover, and that was exactly what Satan had planned for the 21st century. Satan will soon find out, though, that God has a better plan.

CHAPTER 17

GOD'S PLAN

GOD'S PLAN

What exactly is God's plan? I cannot point to one particular passage of Scripture and say, this is God's plan. However, when we read the whole Bible, we find that God's plan revealed in it.

In Genesis chapter 2, we discover that God created the earth and everything in it for mankind. Why is mankind so important? Because mankind, and mankind alone, was created in the image of God, so that we would be able to have fellowship with God. Basically, God's plan is to have a family of adopted sons and daughters who will dwell with Him out of love, and with whom He can have a fellowship that is not possible with the Angels.

Satan seeks an earthly kingdom. He seems to think that if he is able to take over the earth, he will have won. In contrast Jesus said, "My kingdom is not of this world." Those who follow Jesus recognize that they have a dual citizenship. They realize that while they may be called Americans or Canadians or citizens of some other country their eternal citizenship is in heaven. When God's family has reached its full number, the end of this world will come. But before that happens, God has some unfinished business here on this earth.

God's plan for the salvation of mankind was through Abraham. God made some very definite promises and commitments to Abraham.

In Genesis chapter 12, God told Abraham that he would make him a great nation and that he would be a blessing to all the nations of the earth. He also told Abraham in verse three, ***"And I will bless them that bless thee, and curse him that curses thee: and in thee shall all the families of the earth be blessed."*** In Genesis chapter 15, God also gives Abraham the description of the land which he would give to Abraham's descendents.

Some Christians have been taught that since the Jews had rejected Jesus as their Messiah, God had turned to the Gentiles, and that the Christian Church was the New Israel. These Christians are forgetting something. The first Christian churches were all Jewish.

When the apostles went out to preach the gospel, they preached first to the Jews, and then to the Gentiles. The apostle Paul in Romans chapters 10 and 11 makes it very clear that God has not rejected the Jewish people.

In Ezekiel chapters 37, 38, and 39, God shows Ezekiel a vision of how God will restore Israel back to their land. God explains to Ezekiel that when He first brings them back to their land, they will not know Him; but after he has delivered them from their enemies, they will return to Him and worship Him.

In previous chapters we talked about how Israel came back to their land. We realize this came about through the activities of unbelieving Jews, but this is also a part of God's plan. We'll see how all this plays out in the following chapters.

CHAPTER 18

THE 21ST CENTURY

PRESIDENT GEORGE WALKER BUSH (2001 TO 2009)

President Bush in every way has shown himself to be a man of honor and integrity. He has shown himself to be a man with a conscience. He tried to do the things he felt was right even if they were unpopular.

There are those who disparaged his intellectual skills, but the fact of the matter is that he was a graduate of Yale University and Harvard business school where he earned an MBA. He is the only US president to have earned an MBA.

Yet having said all that, while Bush was at Yale University he became a member of the **"Skull and Bones"** society just as his father George HW Bush did before him. The skull and bones society is a secret society connected with the Illuminati. Of course he was also a member of and influenced by the CFR and the elite powers that be.

SEPTEMBER 11, 2001

On the morning of September 11, 2001, nineteen Al Qaeda terrorists hijacked four commercial passenger jets. Two of the planes were deliberately crashed into the twin towers of the World Trade Center in New York. One was crashed into the Pentagon and the other plane crashed into a field in Pennsylvania.

That evening President Bush addressed the nation. He promised a strong response to the attacks. He also emphasized the need for the nation to come together and comfort the families of the victims. On September 14, he visited ground zero and met with Mayor Rudy Giuliani, the firefighters, police officers and volunteers. He then grabbed a bullhorn, while standing on a heap of rubble with the crowd applauding, he said, **"I can hear you. The rest of the world hears you. And the people who knocked these buildings down will hear all of us soon."**

It was quickly determined that Osama bin Laden was the one who had planned that event. President Bush called on the Afghan Taliban regime to turn over Osama bin Laden. When they did not do so, Bush announced a global **"War on Terrorism"** and ordered the invasion of Afghanistan.

President Bush, calling it a **"War on Terrorism"** made a terrible mistake. It is impossible to fight a war on terrorism because terrorism is a technique of warfare. You have to turn your guns against the terrorists. But, who are the terrorists? President Bush finally identified them as being extreme Islamic jihadists. Bush took great pains to announce that we were not at war against Muslims and Islam. He then began a strange form of rhetoric. He said that the threat of terrorism was a threat to our freedom, and that we would have to go to war indefinitely to protect our freedom.

Unfortunately, President Bush was ignoring two facts. Fact number one, terrorists don't want our freedom -- they want our life. Fact number two, Islamic Jihad is a normal part of the Muslim religion and is authorized by their holy book, the Koran. According to the Koran, if Muslims are living in the country where they are in the minority, they are to live peacefully with their neighbors. However, if there is an opportunity to become dominant, they are to use holy jihad to achieve that end, which includes terrorism.

I don't know whether President Bush just didn't want to offend the Muslims dwelling in America and in the Middle East or whether he didn't want to offend the elite powers that be. In any case he stubbornly defended his statements in spite of the fact that Dr. Franklin Graham and others tried to confront him with the truth. He had to know that what he was saying was a lie but he stuck with it anyway.

In any case, Satanic Progressive organizations such as the CFR had determined many years before that they would bring Muslims into the United States in order to counteract Christian influence. No way could President Bush now come out against Muslims.

AFGHANISTAN

On October 7, 2001, U.S. and Australian forces began bombing campaigns in Afghanistan. On November 13 troops were on the ground. In December the Pentagon reported that the Taliban had been defeated.

Efforts to kill or capture Osama bin Laden had failed. Bush said they would continue to weaken the Taliban and Al Qaeda leaders and take out Osama. Their goal was to establish a democratic government in Afghanistan.

IRAQ

In Bush's 2002 State of the Union address he focused attention on Iraq and North Korea, which he labeled the **"axis of evil"**.

He said they were allied with terrorists and posed a grave and growing danger to the United States because of their possession of weapons of mass destruction.

Bush received heavy criticism for his charges that Saddam Hussein had weapons of mass destruction, but reports from the CIA and the past administration testified to that opinion.

Bush urged the United Nations to enforce Iraqi disarmament mandates. Saddam Hussein refused to allow UN weapons inspectors into Iraq.

On March 20, 2003, the United States and 20 other nations invaded Iraq. The Iraqi military was quickly defeated and Baghdad fell on the 9th of April.

On May 1, Bush declared the end of major military combat operations. In January 2005, free democratic elections were held in Iraq for the first time in 50 years.

Saddam Hussein went into hiding, but was later captured and put on trial. It would be wonderful if we could say, "Great job, say goodbye and come home."

Unfortunately things are not quite so simple. There were still many tribal and religious rivalries going on in Iraq. Iran and Al Qaeda were still sending people into Iraq to stir up trouble and fight against the Americans. On January 10, 2007, Bush addressed the nation from the Oval Office and announced a surge of 21,500 more troops in Iraq. He also proposed a jobs program for Iraqis and more reconstruction projects to help rebuild the country.

On July 31, 2008, Bush announced that the surge had been successful and the death of American troops had now reached their lowest number since the beginning of the war in 2003. Due to increased stability in Iraq, Bush also announced the withdrawal of additional American forces.

THE ECONOMY

President Bush was plagued by economic problems from the day he walked into the White House until the day he left. The very nature of fractional reserve banking automatically pulls money out of the economy through the payment of interest. When enough money is pulled out the economy, everything begins to slow down. A correction is about to take place and many businesses that are not strong enough will go bankrupt and will not be able to pay the banks that loaned them money. In order to keep this from happening, the Federal Reserve has been lowering the interest rates and inflating the money supply. The result of their manipulations was to simply put off the day of reckoning. But the day of reckoning always comes. It came in the 1930s with the Great Depression. And it came again in 1971 when Pres. Nixon closed the gold window. If he had not done so, the gold would have quickly left Fort Knox for other countries. So, why was this? It was because the money supply had been so inflated that it was worth less and gold was now worth far more than $35 an ounce.

In 1989, 747 savings and loan associations went bankrupt with losses of $160.1 billion. $124.6 billion of that money was paid by the US government. The Savings and Loan Crisis, in addition to the fact that George HW Bush raised taxes, brought on a mild recession. The country was just coming out of a recession when Bill Clinton became President.

There were several times during the Clinton Administration when the country was coming into a recession. Each time the chairman of the Federal Reserve, Alan Greenspan, dropped the interest rates and inflated the money supply. Inflation in the money supply is accomplished by loaning money into existence, which is created out of thin air by simply running the printing press. The money supply is increased but the goods and services remain the same, therefore the cost of everything in dollar terms is bound to go up.

During the Clinton Administration this money began to flow into technology stocks without regard to whether these companies were actually making any profit, because speculators thought they would in the future and they would be able to sell the stocks for a profit. The result is what has been called the **"dot-com bubble"**. The "dot-com bubble" is just like all other bubbles. Sooner or later they always pop; and when they do it is impossible to blow them back up again.

Alan Greenspan realized that his easy money policy had caused a bubble to form. In order to counteract the speculation he increased interest rates six times during 1999 and early 2000.

The inevitable was bound to happen. On March 10, 2000 the bubble burst. In just six days, the NASDAQ lost 9% going from about 5050 on March 10 to 4580 on March 15.

By 2001, when George W. Bush was President the bubble was deflating at full speed. A majority of the dot-com companies ceased trading. Many of them had never made a profit. Investors now referred to these dot-coms as dot-bombs. By October 2002, the stock market had lost $5 trillion in market value. This meant that George Bush would start out his administration with a recession on his hands.

If that wasn't enough of an economic blow, a second one soon followed. On September 11, 2001, Islamic terrorists flew airliners into the World Trade Center and the Pentagon. This attack was not only an economic blow but also precipitated a war.

President Bush realized that he was now facing an economic recession and also had a war to fight. He went to Congress with a plan to overcome the recession, but the democratically controlled Congress would not go along. He then began to hold town hall style meetings across the United States in order to gain public support for his plan to cut taxes and to give unspent government money back to the people. He argued that tax cuts would stimulate the economy and create jobs. He was finally able to achieve some tax cuts and the economy did grow, although it was at a slower rate than the usual business recovery.

Alan Greenspan also did his thing. He helped to fight the recession by lowering interest rates and running the printing press. The problem is that while Greenspan's easy money policy did help ease the recession, it just began to blow up another bubble. This time it was the housing bubble.

Whenever a government or central bank tries to fight a recession by increasing the money supply, at first it works really well. Just a little bit of inflation stimulates the economy. But later on, it takes a lot of inflation just increase the economy a little bit. You see people get used to inflation. If you do nothing with your money, it will soon be worth half of what it used to be. If you buy bonds or put it into savings, the amount of interest you get will not keep up with the depreciation of your money. The only way to try to come out ahead is to buy stocks, commodities, or real estate and hope it goes up in price. That is the way bubbles are created and why they are created.

Although many people have their own reasons for claiming there was no housing bubble, it was perfectly obvious for anyone who had eyes to see. There were a number of economists who warned about the housing bubble and the risk of subprime mortgages, but they were not heeded. From 2004 to 2006, the Federal Reserve and the government lending agencies, Freddie Mac and Fannie Mae, made it very easy to obtain housing loans. The interest rate on mortgages were so low that everyone wanted to refinance and when they did, they usually took out enough extra money to pay off all their credit cards, which they usually loaded back up again. Homeowners began to use their mortgages like an ATM machine. Speculators also bid houses up in competition with one another, not for the purpose of living in them, but to sell at a profit.

As early as 2003, the Bush administration pushed for significantly increased regulation of Fannie Mae and Freddie Mac. After two years, the regulations finally passed in the House, but the bill died in the Senate. Democratic Senators Barney Frank and Chris Dodd claimed that Fannie Mae and Freddie Mac's lending policies were just fine. They happened to be in bed with political interests that wanted to get poor people into houses they could not afford.

The "Economist" magazine stated, "The worldwide rise in house prices is the biggest bubble in history." A May 2006 Fortune magazine report on the housing bubble stated, "The great housing bubble has finally started to deflate."

In March 2007, national home sales and prices both fell dramatically with the steepest plunge since the 1989 Savings and Loan crisis. By December of that year, it was recognized that the United States was entering a housing market correction and a subprime mortgage crisis, with soaring oil prices. In February 2008, 63,000 jobs were lost. In order to help the situation, Bush signed a $170 billion economic stimulus package in which tax rebate checks were sent to many Americans, and also tax breaks were given to struggling businesses. By September, the crisis became much more serious. The government took over Fannie Mae and Freddie Mac, but let Lehman Brothers collapse. Many people in and out of government concluded that this situation was the worst financial crisis since the Great Depression.

In November 2008, over 500,000 jobs were lost. The Bureau of Labor Statistics reported that in the last four months of 2008, 1.9 million jobs were lost. By the end of 2008, the US had lost a total of 2.6 million jobs.

HURRICANE KATRINA

On August 29, 2005, Hurricane Katrina made landfall. The levies failed and most of New Orleans was flooded. New Orleans and much of the US Gulf Coast was devastated. President Bush was heavily criticized because federal agencies did not move fast enough to manage the disaster. Certainly the Department of Homeland Security and FEMA should have moved faster and more efficiently, but part of the blame has to go to the governor of Louisiana and the mayor of New Orleans, who also dragged their feet.

ENVIRONMENTAL AND ENERGY POLICIES

President Bush took a middle-of-the-road, common sense type of approach to the environment and energy. Bush said he believed that global warming was real but he was not at all sure that it was man-made. He opposed the Kyoto Protocol, which sought to impose mandatory targets to reduce greenhouse gases. This Protocol exempted eighty percent of the world's population while it would have cost the United States tens of billions of dollars per year.

President Bush was also for clean air, clean water, and conservation. In his 2007 State of the Union address, he pledged to try and reduce our reliance upon foreign oil by increasing alternative fuel production. In 2008 Bush lifted the ban on offshore drilling, but Congress also would have to act, because there was still a federal law banning offshore drilling. Bush said, "This means that the only thing standing between the American people and these vast oil reserves is action from the U.S. Congress." Bush also supported other gas saving technologies like advanced batteries and hydrogen fuel cells.

IMMIGRATION

In 2006, Bush urged Congress to allow more than 12 million illegal immigrants to work in the United States with the creation of a temporary guest worker program.

While he did not support amnesty, he argued that the lack of legal status denies millions of people the protection of US laws and penalized employers who needed immigrant labor. He also urged Congress to provide additional funds for border security and to deploy 6000 National Guard troops for that purpose. This proposal failed mainly because people no longer trusted the government to do what they said they would do. People demanded that the border be secured first.

EDUCATION, HEALTH, AND SOCIAL SECURITY

Early in his presidency Bush signed into law the No Child Left behind Act. He felt that every child had to be provided every opportunity to succeed. This act provided for testing of children and other incentives to help bring educational opportunities of the poor to that of more affluent areas.

President Bush was also very much pro-life. He strongly supported the Partial Birth Abortion Ban. While he supported adult stem cell research he refused to support any kind of embryonic stem cell research which called for the death of an embryo. He did, however lift the ban on research of 71 existing lines of stem cells. On July 19 2006, Bush vetoed the Stem Cell Research Enhancement Act. That legislation would have allowed federal money to be used for research where stem cells are derived from the destruction of an embryo. By the way, adult stem cell research has shown a great deal of promise, but no medical progress has been made from the research of embryonic cells.

As an aid to seniors, President Bush signed into law the Medicare prescription drug benefit act and tried to reform Social Security, but the political will of Congress was simply not there.

APPROVAL RATINGS

Bush began his presidency with an approval rating near 50%. After the attacks of September 11, 2001 his approval rating went to 90% and it remained over 50% during most of his first term in office. During his second term in office, however, he began to receive heavy criticism for his handling of the Iraq war and his response to Hurricane Katrina and other controversies. Polls conducted in 2006 showed that his approval ratings had gone down to 37%. There were times in his presidency that his approval rating dropped much lower and he left the White House as one of America's most unpopular presidents.

It is my opinion that President Bush is a good man who tried to the best of his ability to do what is right. He is far smarter than most of his critics and if the America that we have known and loved still exists 25 years from now, President Bush's popularity will be far greater than it is now.

CHAPTER 19

THE BEGINNING OF THE END?

BARAK HUSSEIN OBAMA II (2009 --_____)

He claims to have been born August 4, 1961 at one of the hospitals in Hawaii. He does have a certificate of live birth from Hawaii, but this certificate is also issued to people that were born in other places but lived in Hawaii. No long form birth certificate showing the hospital where he was born, and the doctor who delivered him has never been produced for public view. Finally, after Donald Trump said that he was going to personally investigate Obama's birth and Dr. Jerome Corsi's book called "Where's the Birth Certificate" was about to be released, the White House hastily presented a computer generated representation of a Hawaii Birth Certificate. Computer experts have said that it was produced by copying at least two different birth certificates and by doing a lot of copy and paste. In some cases they used computer fonts to put it all together. Needless to say, the original birth certificate has never been seen. Without question the Birth Certificate that Obama has produced is a fraud.

If it is true that Obama's birth certificate is a fraud, why haven't the news media exposed it? Even Fox News has refused to even consider it. Why haven't members of Congress looked into it? Why, won't the US Courts considered it? Could they possibly be so naïve as to think that what Obama has said and written must be true because he said it? Or are they afraid? Are they afraid of being accused of being racists? Are they afraid that race riots might occur if he is challenged? Or could it be that they are so afraid of the powers that be that they don't dare challenge Obama in this way?

Actually many people have challenged Obama, but no one with enough power to do anything about it. When they try to challenge Obama in the courts, the courts refuse to hear the case.

Many people have questioned where he was born. His African grandmother once stated that she was present at his birth in Kenya. Later it has been said that she did not understand the translators at the time and has now denied that he was born in Kenya however there are a large number of Kenyans who believe he was born there. Not only that but she repeatedly proclaimed that she was present at his birth. Where was that? It couldn't have been in Hawaii because she had never been there.

The Constitution of the United States requires that a president of the United States must be a natural born citizen. That means one born either in the United States or any territory of the United States. The Constitution also prohibits a president of the United States from having a dual citizenship or undue influence from a foreign country.

Obama's father was a native of Kenya, which at that time, was the territory of Great Britain. If he was born in Kenya, he could be considered a Kenyan and a British citizen.

His mother, Stanley Ann Dunham, was born in Wichita, Kansas. His parents met in a Russian language class at the

University of Hawaii in 1960. His parents married on February 2, 1961, but were separated when Obama Senior went to Harvard University on a scholarship. They were divorced in 1964.

After the divorce, Obama's mother married an Indonesian student named Lolo Soetoro, who was attending college in Hawaii. Indonesian students were recalled and the family moved to Jakarta, Indonesia. From ages 6 to 10, Obama attended schools in Jakarta, where he studied the Koran and was considered a Muslim. During this time he went by the name of Barry Sorrento. In 1971 he returned to Honolulu, Hawaii to live with his mother's parents. In 1981, he went to Columbia University and then to Harvard Law School.

During the time that Obama was running for Congress and then later for President of the United States, his citizenship has never been properly vetted.

An article by Bob Unruh, posted on WorldNetDaily. com, September 25, 2010 says, "It long has been documented that when Barack Obama was picked by the Democratic Party to be its 2008 presidential candidate, only one state - Hawaii - was sent a document from Nancy Pelosi certifying that he was qualified under the requirements of the U.S. Constitution." The original report of this came from J.B. Williams, a commentator at the Canada Free Press who stated that the Democrats failed to certify their candidate's eligibility in 49 of 50 states. He also stated, "It appears that the DNC never certified the constitutional eligibility for Barak Hussein Obama, despite their many claims of proper vetting and certification, all of which we now know is false."

Williams also released copies of two documents apparently prepared by Democrats to certify Obama as their nominee.

One contains language affirming his constitutional eligibility, filed in Hawaii where state law requires the specific language, and another omits the language, filed in the remaining 49 states.

In choosing Al Gore and Joe Lieberman in 2000, this was their statement:

> "THIS IS TO CERTIFY that the following candidates for President and Vice-President of the United States are legally qualified to serve under the provisions of the United States Constitution and are the duly chosen candidates of both the state and the national Democratic Parties by balloting at the Presidential Preference Poll and Caucus held March 7, 2000 in the State of Hawaii and by acclamation at the National Democratic Convention held August 14-17, 2000 in Los Angeles, California."

The wording was almost identical on behalf of John Kerry and John Edwards in 2004, but in 2008, the wording is changed.

> "THIS IS TO CERTIFY that the following candidates for President and Vice President of the United States are legally qualified to serve under the provisions of the national Democratic Parties balloting at the Presidential Preference Poll and Caucus held on February 19th, 2008, in the State of Hawaii and by acclamation at the National Democratic Convention held August 27, 2009, in Denver, Colorado."

What the Democratic Party of Hawaii's 2008 Certification of Nomination left out are these words: ***"of the United States Constitution and are the duly chosen candidates of both the state and,"***

By omitting the above words, the Democratic Party of Hawaii merely certified that Obama was legally qualified to serve as president because he received most of the ballots in the Democratic Parties Primaries in 50 states. They did not make the claim that Obama is legally qualified to serve as president under the provisions of the U.S. Constitution!

They also did not say that Obama and Biden were the chosen candidates of the state of Hawaii.

The Hawaii Democratic Party also ignored their protocols of 2008 in order to not certify Obama's eligibility as they had done for candidates in previous elections.

Even though many questions were raised about Obama's eligibility, Obama would not share any of his personal records such as his birth, baptism, school, college, medical, or passports. Moreover, no one who was eligible to challenge his eligibility would do so. Anyone who should have been able to challenge him was dismissed by the courts that refused to get involved.

Nevertheless, in the 2008 general election Obama defeated John McCain and was inaugurated as President of the United States on January 20, 2009. Now let's see who he is and what he has done as President of the United States.

WHO IS HE?

While we don't know everything about his birth or citizenship we do know quite a bit about his upbringing, education, and the people who influenced him. We may not be able to accurately define him, but there are some very interesting questions we might ask, based on what we do know.

1. What is his religion? Is he a Muslim?
    We know that his mother was not religious and that his father was a Muslim. When

his mother remarried, she again married a Muslim. We know that he was brought up as a Muslim in Indonesia and studied the Koran. We also know that anyone brought up as a Muslim is considered to be a Muslim for life, and Obama is so regarded in Muslim countries. We have also seen him bow before Muslim rulers.

2. Is he a Christian?

He claims that he read some of the precepts of Jesus and converted to Christianity and joined Jeremiah Wright's church, Trinity United Church of Christ, which he attended for about 20 years. We also know that lying is considered acceptable for a Muslim who is living in a Christian country if it is done for a good reason.

Wright's church was considered the place to be for upward mobility in the Chicago black community and would help Obama connect with other black churches in his organizing efforts. Wright's messages were hate filled rants spouting black liberation theology which can hardly be called Christian. So even if Obama was sincere, there is still a huge question as to whether he is a Christian.

3. Is he a Progressive, Socialist or a Communist?

We know that in Hawaii where he spent most of his years growing up his mentor was a Communist. We also know by his own words in what he has written that he actively sought out socialists and communists for his friends and associates. We also know that since he has become President, that almost all of his advisors and associates are Progressives, Socialists, or Communists.

4. Is Obama trying to fulfill an anti-colonial dream?

Obama wrote a book called "Dreams from My Father". It is an autobiography in which he tries to find out who he really is. He even goes to Kenya to discover his roots and to understand the thinking of his father. His father was the son of a resister of colonial rule by the British and had been arrested and tortured by them.

Dinesh D'Souza also wrote a book called, "The Roots of Obama's Rage." D'Souza explains that Obama is a man driven by the anti-colonial ideology of his father. This is the real reason why he had the bust of Winston Churchill packed up and sent back to England. He still has an inherited rage against the British for their colonial rule and for torturing his grandfather.

Obama actually seeks to reduce America's strength, influence, and standard of living because he believes that America needs to share all that it has with the rest of the world.

5. Who is he really?

We still don't know. He certainly does not appear to be a Christian and perhaps not a Muslim either. Maybe he is just a pragmatist who says and does whatever is necessary to satisfy his ambitions.

We know that he has been immersed in progressive, socialist and communist ideology, but we don't know what he really believes. We do know that he uses these people to carry out his agenda and seems to go along with their thinking.

There are some things that we do know about him. He is highly intelligent, pragmatic, ruthless, determined, and dangerous; perhaps far more dangerous than anyone can imagine. Would he try to create a crisis so that he could convince the American people that things were now so dangerous it is necessary to establish "Martial Law" and use this to establish a dictatorship? We just don't know.

WHAT DID HE DO BEFORE BECOMING PRESIDENT?

From June 1985 to May 1988 he was hired as director of the Developing Communities Project, a church-based community organization in Chicago. His job was to organize the community in setting up a job training program, a college preparatory tutoring program, and a tenants' rights organization. He also worked as a consultant and instructor for another community organizing institute, the Gamaliel Foundation.

In mid-1988, he travelled to Europe and then to Kenya to visit his father's birthplace and meet his relatives. Later that year, he entered Harvard Law School, where he earned his law degree and wrote "Dreams from My Father."

After this he was associated with The University of Chicago Law School where he served as a Lecturer from 1996 to 2004. He also practiced law during most of this time as a civil rights attorney.

In 1992, Obama directed Illinois's Project Vote. This was a voter registration drive with ten staffers and seven hundred volunteer registrars. It achieved its goal of registering 150,000 of 400,000 unregistered African Americans in the state.

From 1994 to 2002, Obama served on the boards of directors of various organizations such as the "Woods Fund of Chicago, The Joyce Foundation and the Chicago Annenberg Challenge."

WHAT HAS HE DONE SINCE BECOMING PRESIDENT?

From his first day in office Obama has committed himself to fulfill his campaign pledge to fundamentally transform and remake America. Most people who voted for him thought that he meant that he would correct abuses, right wrongs, make improvements and restore America to what it ought to be, but that's not what he meant. When he said that he would fundamentally transform America that is exactly what he meant. While Obama would continue to say many things that the American people wanted to hear, his actions would say something different.

THE MILITARY

Obama appears to want to make the United States military equal to the other nations of the world. In order for this to happen, the United States would have to lose its superpower status. Obama wasted no time. In his first few days in office Obama issued executive orders and presidential memoranda directing the U.S. military to develop plans to withdraw troops from Iraq and ordered the closing of the Guantanamo Bay detention camp as soon as it could be arranged.

On February 27, 2009, Obama declared that combat operations would end in Iraq within 18 months. By the end of August 2010 combat operations officially ended. The troops remaining in Iraq would be to train, equip and advise Iraqi security forces. Some of the Iraqi security forces had already started to defect to Al Qaeda.

During the 2008 presidential campaign, Obama referred to the Iraq war as the bad war and declared that we needed to turn our attention to Afghanistan. Since then he has increased troop levels in Afghanistan. The situation grew worse instead of better.

They would like to withdraw from Afghanistan but cannot do so without admitting failure. The Afghan government is corrupt. Many of the enemy fighters and supplies come through Pakistan. The Pakistani government is not fully stable, but they have considerable nuclear weapons. If the Taliban and Al Qaeda take over Pakistan, these nuclear weapons would fall into the hands of terrorists. Obama now finds himself in a dilemma. He can't withdraw the way he would like to, nor does he find himself in a position to win the war in Afghanistan.

In spite of all of this, he continues to try to weaken the military by unilaterally cutting our nuclear weapons and has now mandated that homosexuals to be able to openly serve in the military.

THE ECONOMY

In February 2009, Obama signed the $787 billion economic stimulus bill into law. Before the bill was passed, Obama repeatedly talked about all the shovel ready jobs that would be created. He declared that without the stimulus bill, the unemployment rate would go up to 8.6%. Since the bill has been passed and signed into law, the unemployment rate officially went up to 9.6% and most of the money was spent on social programs or went to the unions that supported him. About two years later Obama admitted that there is no such thing as shovel ready jobs.

In March 2009, Obama talked with automobile industry executives. Ford, GM and Chrysler were having financial difficulties partly due to the recession and partly due to concessions they had been forced to make to the unions. General Motors and Chrysler accepted loans from the government while they were trying to get their businesses reorganized. Ford Motor Company refused all loans. The White House then set terms for the bankruptcy of General Motors and Chrysler. They decided to sell Chrysler to the Italian automaker Fiat. They then gave the US government a 60% stake in the equity of General Motors and gave the Canadian government a 12% stake. This left the common shareholders with a 28% stake, while the preferred shareholders were paid nothing. The auto unions though, made out like bandits. They were fully rewarded for their support of Obama.

Obama really meant it when he said that he wanted to redistribute the wealth. A lot of poor people in the United States think that redistributing the wealth is a great idea. They like the idea of getting some of the rich people's money. What they don't understand is that Obama is not talking about giving them the rich people's money. What he is talking about is taking the wealth of America and giving it to all of the poor countries of the world. We can see this more clearly as we look at the oil spill in the Gulf of Mexico.

On April 20, 2010, an explosion destroyed the Deepwater Horizon drilling rig in the Gulf of Mexico. Obama began a federal investigation, formed a bipartisan commission to recommend new safety standards, and on May 27 he announced a six-month moratorium on all new deepwater drilling permits and visas. Behind the scenes, however, Obama's administrators refused even shallow water drilling permits.

Louisiana Gov. Bobby Jindal said that the newest threat to the economy of the state is Pres. Barack Obama's moratorium on deepwater drilling. He said that this would turn an environmental disaster into an economic catastrophe for his state. Every day the moratorium was in effect cost the State untold millions of dollars. Jindal pointed out that studies showed that within five months, the moratorium will result in a layoff of 3,339 Louisiana workers and a loss of 7,656 additional jobs, while the state expected to lose more than 20,000 existing and potential new jobs over the next 12 to 18 months.

According to Burt Adams of the National Ocean Industries Association, more than 200,000 jobs were tied to the offshore drilling industry and 35,000 workers were directly involved each day when the rigs were in use. The American Petroleum Institute forecasted that if the drilling ban were to continue, more than 120,000 jobs would be lost in the Gulf Coast and key resources abandoned or moved elsewhere.

It is very costly for deep drilling rigs to stand idle, up to $100,000 a day. Some of them moved to Brazil. The

Obama administration actually gave money to Brazil to encourage their oil exploration. Could that have been because Obama's friend George Soros, had money invested in deep rig oil drilling?

If the drilling moratorium had anything to do with safety as they claim, why would the Obama administration hold up permits for shallow water drilling that doesn't have the same safety consequences? And why would he subsidize drilling in Brazil where the wells would be twice as deep as the Deepwater Horizon?

The truth is the moratorium had absolutely nothing to do with safety of the environment or for the concerns of the workers, jobs, or the economy of the Gulf Coast. Instead Obama had other concerns. He actually rejoices at the thought of oil becoming scarce and expensive. He wants to move America away from a fossil-based energy economy to a renewable energy economy. At the same time, he seems to have no concern at all about the pain and suffering of the American people. Nor does he seem to be concerned that America's energy will have to be supplied by people who hate us. After all, the American people will have to learn how to share their riches with the rest of the world.

In the meantime, the economy has not recovered in spite of the stimulus plan and $3 trillion deficit spending. At this time under Obama leadership the National debt has doubled that of all the Presidents before him to almost 18 Trillion Dollars.

Officially the unemployment rate is somewhere close to 10%, but unofficially it is actually closer to 25% of unemployed and discouraged workers.

HEALTH CARE

One of Obama's key campaign promises was to improve healthcare for everyone. He called upon Congress to pass legislation reforming health care. On July 14, 2009, House Democratic leaders introduced a 1017 page plan for overhauling the US healthcare system. This legislation was not written by Congress, but by progressive think tanks of Obama's choosing. The bill was never debated openly in Congress but only behind closed doors in Democratic conference rooms. Speaker of the House Pelosi said that they would have to pass it in order to find out what was in it.

In spite of the fact that the bill had no Republican supporters and was against the will of the American people, the Democratic leaders rammed the bill through Congress. Obama quickly signed the bill into law on March 23, 2010.

The so-called healthcare law also called Obamacare is a monstrosity. It takes away money from Medicare and will lead to rationing of care for the elderly. If it is not completely repealed it will destroy all private health insurance and will eventually bring all medical care under government control. It will surely succeed in making healthcare in America the equal of Great Britain and Canada, far inferior to what we have had in the past. This healthcare law has got to be repealed. At this point though it can not simply be repealed, it has to be replaced with something better.

CHAPTER 20

WHERE DO WE GO FROM HERE?

Ps 11:3 If the foundations be destroyed,

what can the righteous do?

Pr 14:34 Righteousness exalts a nation:

But sin is a reproach to any people.

America has entered one of the most dangerous times in its history. There are people who are working night and day to turn our country into just another state of the New World Order. These people fervently believe in what they are doing. They are extremely dangerous and must be resisted by every means possible.

The term New World order is not new by any means. Ever since Freemasonry was co-opted by Adam Weishaupt, this term has been used to signify the coming world government over which Antichrist would rule. One of the illuminated Freemasonry's sacred symbols portraying this message was placed on the back of the one dollar bill by Pres. Franklin D. Roosevelt. This Masonic symbol contains a pyramid with the all seeing eye of Osiris above it. Underneath the pyramid is written in Latin "Novus Ordo Seclorum" which means the New Order of the Ages or The New World Order. This symbol was designed by Masons and became the reverse side of the great seal of the United States in 1782. What was on the reverse side of the seal was not secret but not many people knew about it for more than 150 years until it was placed on the one dollar bill. Notice that the capstone is separated from the rest of the pyramid; this signifies that the New World order is not yet complete. Once the New World order has been built, the capstone will be joined to the rest of the pyramid.

THE STRUCTURE OF THE NEW WORLD ORDER

Picture in your mind the New World Order as a building in process of being built, supported by four pillars. These four pillars are: the Political, the Military, the Economic, and the Religious Pillars. If any of these pillars are removed, the New World order will fall down. These pillars are still in construction. As soon as these pillars are complete, the New World order can be built upon it.

The Political Pillar is almost complete. Various people in history have tried to build this political pillar in order to establish a world empire. Napoleon tried but failed. Hitler tried but he failed. Woodrow Wilson got the League of Nations going, but the United States refused to join it. Finally in 1945, the United Nations was born with the United States as one of its charter members. The United Nations and its various organizations form the structure upon which the world government can be built.

The Military Pillar still has a ways to go. The goal is to bring all the military powers of the world under the United Nations. In order for this to happen, the superpower status of the United States must be eliminated. Obama is already doing all he can to make that happen. There have already been attempts to take certain military actions under the banner of the United Nations, but only a few nations actually took part in it. Much construction is still needed to make the military pillar a reality.

The Economic Pillar seems to be just about ready to go as soon as the signal is given. For over half a century the United States dollar has been the reserve currency of the world, but during that time the dollar has been constantly devalued and systematically destroyed. I do not believe this was done by accident or by stupidity. It has been planned this way, because the dollar has to be destroyed in order to get the world to switch over to a New World Order Monetary System. The United States debt is almost $18 trillion. At this point, I believe the biggest problem the powers that be have is to keep the dollar from crashing before it's time.

The Religious Pillar is designed to coerce all religions of the world to become one. Christians, Jews, and Muslims can never truly be assimilated as long as they keep their religious differences. These religious differences must be overcome for them to unite under the New World order. The powers that be have tried various methods to break down Christian faith and values. They have seen to it that our new teachers are trained in progressive education. These teachers then teach the progressive line intended to confuse the children and to destroy their Christian faith. Some of these things are:

1. The teaching of evolution in the public schools.
2. They try to remove all objective standards for right and wrong. They claim that people set the standard for what is right and wrong, not God.

3. They promote gender confusion in children. They promote masculine roles for girls and feminine roles for boys.
4. They started off teaching sex education, and then they started teaching about sex, and how to avoid pregnancy and abortion.
5. Progressives want to get rid of the family. Therefore they must get rid of traditional marriage. Progressive teachers now claim that a family is made up of people who love one another and want to live with each other. It could be composed of a man, a woman and children; or it could be composed of two men and children or two women and children.
6. They began to promote a homosexual lifestyle. They told the boys that they might really be a girl in a boy's body and they told little girls that they might really be a boy in a girl's body. But, that's okay because they were just born that way. In this way they take little children who are trying to find their own identities and mix them up even more.

Since Satan is the one who is behind the Illuminati, the Progressives, the Globalists, Witches, Warlocks, Occultists, and all the pagan religions, it is only natural that they would find common ground together. Satan and the New World Order are not that concerned about integrating these people into the one world religion. They don't even consider Islam to be a problem. It is Christianity that must be destroyed. For that reason, they have introduced substitute religions and used many organizations for that purpose.

MOTHER EARTH RELIGION.

The idea of mother Earth goes back to antiquity, but there is now a new twist on it. James Lovelock, a NASA astrophysics came up with the idea that the Earth is a living being that is in the process of becoming self-aware. He called this the Gaia Hypothesis. He said that Mother Earth is a virgin and that she is immortal. She is the mother of us all, but she is not a tolerant mother. He goes on to say that if we hinder her objectives, she will eliminate us without pity. This fits in nicely with the occult and all other heathen religions.

NEW AGE RELIGIONS

New Age Religions are compatible with the occult, witchcraft, and Mother Earth. Many New Age Religions speak of Christ consciousness and Christ in you. When they speak of Christ in you, they are not talking about Jesus in your heart. Instead, they are talking about a Christ consciousness, or a god consciousness. In other words you are Christ, you are a little god.

In Elbert County, Georgia, there is a granite monument called the Georgia Guidestones. It is almost 20 feet tall and weighs over 245,000 pounds. It displays the New Age 10 Commandments written in eight languages. The donor remains anonymous, but it is thought that perhaps Ted Turner, the founder of CNN, may be responsible for it. These Guidestones do not specify a supreme being but do pretty well capture the spirit of the new age.

1. Maintain humanity under 500,000,000 in perpetual balance with nature.
2. Guide reproduction wisely - improving fitness and diversity.

3. Unite humanity with a living new language.
4. Rule passion - faith - tradition - and all things with tempered reason.
5. Protect people and nations with fair laws and just courts.
6. Let all nations rule internally resolving external disputes in a world court.
7. Avoid petty laws and useless officials.
8. Balance personal rights with social duties.
9. Prize truth - beauty - love - seeking harmony with the infinite.
10. Be not a cancer on the earth - – Leave room for nature – Leave room for nature.

ENVIRONMENTALISM

Environmentalism is a false religion. They are very concerned about air pollution, water pollution, and the extinction of plants and animals. Christians also should be concerned about the environment because God has made us caretakers of His creation, but that is not what environmentalism is all about. Environmentalists are not Christians, but Mother Earth worshipers. They see mankind as the destroyers of the earth. They consider man to be a virus upon the earth.

GLOBAL WARMING

Global Warming is a hoax. In the 1970s and 80s people were saying that the earth was cooling, and if we didn't do something about pollution, we were going to enter a new Ice Age. But in the 1990s, sunspot activity increased and the earth actually warmed slightly. Therefore the coming Ice Age scare wouldn't work anymore. It was now necessary to change the message.

The new message is that air pollution and greenhouse gases are going to cause the earth to get so hot that the polar ice caps will melt and the world will be flooded. They used lots of scientific data and temperature measurements to prove their point. The problem is that it has now been proven that their temperature measurements are inaccurate and their so-called scientific data has been manipulated to make it appear that the earth is warming. The reason why they did all this is so that the powers that be might be able to enact laws and regulations which would give them control of the resources of the earth.

THE CULT OF DEATH

The Cult of Death is not an organized religion but arises from the belief that man is a virus upon the earth; and that in order for the earth to be healed, man must either be eliminated or their numbers greatly reduced.

A French oceanographer, Jacques Cousteau, wrote an article which appeared in the November 1991 edition of UNESCO Courier in which he stated: "to stabilize world population we must eliminate 350,000 people per day. It is a horrible thing to say, but it's just as bad not to say it."

The first commandment of the Georgia guide stones which we quoted previously says, "Maintain humanity under 500,000,000 in perpetual balance with nature."

There are approximately 7,000,000,000 people. According to the Georgia guides stones. In order to reduce the population down to 500,000,000 would mean that for every 14 people that are living today it would be necessary to get rid of 13 to reach that goal.

How could they do that? Wouldn't the people rebel and defend themselves? Of course they would if they understood

WHERE DO WE GO FROM HERE?

what was happening. However, there is a way to kill people off without them even realizing what is happening.

The powers that be have already started using various methods to try to reduce the population. Some of these are:

1. **Abortion and Infanticide**
2. **Homosexual lifestyle:** Homosexuals do not usually have children.
3. **Promotion of feminism**. Feminists try to convince young women that they should have a career of their own and not be a slave to a husband and a servant to her children.
4. **By withholding food and water** from disabled patients until they die, sometimes by court order.
5. **By promoting euthanasia** like Dr. Jack Kevorkian did when he assisted in over 30 so-called suicides.
6. **Health care reform:** also referred to as Obamacare, which without a doubt will result in the rationing of care to the elderly.
7. **Genetic engineering of food:** experiments have shown that genetically modified corn, soy, and other crops have caused cancerous tumors and all kinds of other problems in animals. What do you think it might be doing to people? Do you think perhaps that might be the reason that the people who are doing these things don't eat their own food but are instead eating organic foods and storing good uncontaminated seed in special vaults frozen in the Arctic?

8. **Genetically modified bacteria and viruses:** These organisms could kill vast numbers of people very quickly, without people even catching on.

9. **Immunizations** could be used to make people sick. Instead of trying to keep them well.

10. **Pharmaceutical companies and the FDA:** They have been trying to keep all natural cures under wraps. They even want to make natural food supplements and vitamins to be bought and sold by prescription only.

11. **Famine:** in order to really kill off the population, all it would take would be a good famine. That really wouldn't be that hard to arrange. It could be something as simple as knocking out the electricity by an EMP (Electro Magnetic Pulse). Without electricity, fresh foods in the grocery stores would soon start spoiling. Furthermore without being able to use debit or credit cards people would very quickly run out of money to buy anything. Even if you had money, the gas stations would not be able to pump gas to put in your car. The use of trucks to bring food into the cities would come to a standstill. The country would pretty much shut down. Riots with people looking for food would soon take place. Martial law would be declared in order to keep order. Half of the American population could be eliminated within two months and about 95% would be dead within a year. That is only

one way to cause death and destruction, there are many other ways.

Do I believe that all these things will actually take place? No I don't, even though they have already been implementing many of these things. In order to properly carry out their plans would require decades. I believe the Lord Jesus will return long before then.

The 10th Commandment on the Georgia guides stones, says, **"Be not a Cancer on the earth - leave room for nature - leave room for nature."**

For some time, environmental groups, and back to nature groups that worship mother Earth have been trying to take land out of production and restore it to nature. This has been going on since the 1970s, but nothing like what has been taking place under Pres. Obama. It is not just a matter of protecting endangered species. Instead, the agenda is to reduce the human population and to make it impossible for people to live in these places. Under the leadership of Obama, the EPA has been trying to shut down the coal mines and electric generating stations that use coal. They are also trying to stop oil refineries from being built, and the drilling of oil and gas to take place. They also refused to allow the Keystone pipeline to be built. Besides taking land and calling it national Parks. The government is now also trying to take control of lots of other property. A law that was designed to regulate Navigable Waters in Rivers is being misinterpreted in order to give the government control of any land on which rain falls and runs into a stream or lake even part of a year. That means that permission is now needed, in many places, to be able to build a house or develop property.

THE FINALE

1. **The Destruction of America:** I believe that the destruction of the United States is at the top of Satan's agenda. The U.S. has to be destroyed. Our Bill of Rights, our Constitution, our Free Enterprise System, our Freedom, our Christianity, the US dollar has to go to make way for the New World Order. The crashing of our monetary system is imminent. Satan's Elite have been pulling the strings of the Politicians in both political parties to get everything ready for the launching of the New World Order. Most of the Politicians who are doing Satan's bidding probably have no idea of the consequences of their actions.

2. **The Crisis, which will be the excuse for Marshall Law:** It could be the crashing of the dollar, a famine, race riots, or a terrorist attack (either real or contrived). Most likely it will be something which causes people to riot in the streets which would cause most people to call for law and order.

3. **Marshall Law:** The actions that have been taken by homeland security and the military indicate that the government intends to bring about Marshall Law.
    a. FEMA prisons have been established throughout the country.
    b. I have seen pictures of mountains of FEMA plastic caskets.

    c.   FEMA and other government agencies are buying as much ammunition and non military weapons as possible in order to keep them off the private market. The only conceivable reason for this is to keep citizens from being able to defend themselves.

    d.   The government has bought 30,000 guillotines.

    e.   The NSA has been monitoring every phone call, email, and every Face Book post. They are even photographing every letter, front and back. We are being monitored by the GPS on our cell phones, our cars, by cameras, license plate readers, by our credit and debit cards. Our cell phones can be activated remotely and they can listen to our conversations even if they are turned off and even our TV's can be used against us. Privacy no longer exists unless one goes to extreme measures to keep off the radar. While it is impossible for any group of human beings to do all this monitoring it isn't too hard for computers to look for key words or key purchases to clue them in on who to monitor more closely.

4. **Powerlessness of Congress:** Satan has his Elites in both the Republican and Democrat parties. There are a few good men and women in Congress, but they are so outnumbered, they are not able to do much about the way the country is going. Many of them talk a good talk but when it comes to doing the things that need to be done, they are missing in action.

5. **Dictatorship:** We were taught in school that America is a Constitutional Republic and that we are governed by the rule of law. In fact, we have a virtual dictatorship, because Congress has refused to act on the behalf of the American People. The Constitution and Law have become simply pieces of paper which Obama and his Attorney Generals decide whether or not they want to abide by.

I have no way of knowing the exact timetable for these events to take place, but when we consider the preparations that have already been made for these events to take place, it would seem that the time is near.

Then when the ruling elite believe that the time is right, there will be a crisis, either real or invented, and the government will say it has to take over for the good of the people. Once this takes place it will be almost impossible to regain freedom without a bloody revolution.

I hate to leave this chapter on such a negative note, but in the next two chapters we will look at what God thinks about all this and what we can do about it.

CHAPTER 21

THE ISRAEL FACTOR

GOD'S PROMISE TO ABRAHAM:

In Genesis chapter 12; 1, 2 God made a promise to Abraham which has never been revoked. *"I will make of thee a great nation, and I will bless thee, and make thy name great; and thou shalt be a blessing: And I will bless them that bless thee, and curse him that curseth thee: and in thee shall all families of the earth be blessed."* That means that even today, this when a nation comes against Israel, God will come against that nation.

THE MIRACLE OF ISRAEL:

In 70 A.D., a Roman general named Titus completely destroyed Jerusalem. The Jews that survived were sold into slavery and scattered all over the world. Ordinarily, when a nation has had that done to them, they would completely disappear within a few generations, except for mention in history books. Yet, for about 2,000 years, the Jewish people never lost their identity. Then, in the 20th century, God begin to fulfill his promise (see Ezekiel chapters 37–38) of bringing them back to their land that he had given them. In 1948, they became a nation and in 1967, they regained the city of Jerusalem. That day the Jews made a vow that the city of Jerusalem would not be divided again.

William Koenig wrote a book in 2004, called "Eye to Eye" which shows what has happened to America each time our government tries to pressure Israel to compromise or make agreements which are harmful to them. Within 24 hours after such hurtful agreements are made, disaster strikes. In 2006 John McTernan wrote a book called, "As America Has Done to Israel" on much the same theme. I highly recommend both of these books. Now Pres. Obama has completely turned his back upon Israel and made a deal with Iran's leaders who have promised to annihilate Israel. If Congress approves this deal, you can be sure that America will suffer for it.

ISRAEL'S END TIME WARS:

In Ezekiel Chapter 37, God shows Ezekiel a field full of dry bones. God explains to Ezekiel that these dry bones represent the house of Israel which would be scattered over all the earth (from 70 A.D. until the 20th century). God asked Ezekiel, *"Son of Man, can these bones live?"* Ezekiel does not know quite what to make of it all and so he replies, *"Oh Lord God you know."* So God tells Ezekiel to prophesy to the bones. After Ezekiel finishes prophesying, the bones come together, the flesh and skin cover them, and they stand up – a great army.

God explains to Ezekiel that even though Israel would be scattered throughout the world and the people would have given up hope of ever coming back to their land, God would bring them back and reestablish them in the land. God also tells Ezekiel that after He has delivered them from their enemies, the people will repent and turn back to Him and He will put His Spirit within them.

In Ezekiel Chapters 38 and 39, God gives Ezekiel a vision of a coming invasion of Israel by the nations that hate her. The invading nations are: Gog, Persia, Ethiopia, Libya, Gomer, Togarmah, and many other people with them. The nations here listed are ancient names of people groups that were living at the time when Ezekiel wrote this prophecy. In order for us to understand who the people are that will be fighting in this war, we need to update these names. Gog is Turkey and Russia. Persia is Iran. Ethiopia and Libya still retain their ancient names. Gomer is Eastern Europe and Togarmah is Turkey, Bosnia and the people around the Black Sea. Many other people with them would no doubt include some of the Arab nations surrounding Israel. Notably absent from this list is Egypt and Assyria which today is Iraq. Perhaps the reason they are not on the list is because they will no longer enemies of Israel.

In Psalm 83 verse 4 we read *"come and let us cut them off from being a nation; that the name of Israel may be no more in remembrance."* In verses 6, 7 and 8 we see that the people who want to cut off Israel from being a nation are the people who live in the modern states of Jordan, Iraq, and Lebanon.

In verses 9 - 18, the psalmist prays that they would be defeated and made like stubble, that their faces might be filled with shame and that they might know that *" thou, whose name alone is Jehovah art the most high over all the Earth."* If God answers the psalmist prayer these nations will no longer be enemies of Israel.

Isaiah chapter 19 deals with Egypt. In Isa 19:1 we read, *"The burden of Egypt. Behold, the LORD rideth upon a swift cloud, and shall come into Egypt: and the idols of Egypt shall be moved at his presence, and the heart of Egypt shall melt in the midst of it."*

First God gets rid of the idols. Then the Egyptians see what God is doing in Israel and they are afraid to come against the counsel of the Lord of hosts as we see in Isaiah 19:16, 17. *"In that day shall Egypt be like unto women: and it shall be afraid and fear because of the shaking of the hand of the LORD of hosts, which he shaketh over it. And the land of Judah shall be a terror unto Egypt, every one that maketh mention thereof shall be afraid in himself, because of the counsel of the LORD of hosts, which he hath determined against it."*

Finally, Egypt turns to the Lord God of Israel and to our Lord Jesus for deliverance and he saves them as we see in Isaiah 19: 19, 20 *"In that day shall there be an altar to the LORD in the midst of the land of Egypt, and a pillar at the border thereof to the LORD. And it shall be for a sign and for a witness unto the LORD of hosts in the land of Egypt: for they shall cry unto the LORD because of the oppressors, and he shall send them a saviour, and a great one, and he shall deliver them."* Therefore they will no longer be enemies of Israel.

God tells Ezekiel that when this invasion takes place, God will fight on Israel's side and this invading force will be defeated. The last verse in Ezekiel 38 says, *"Then they shall know that I am the Lord."*

When will all this happened? I don't know for sure but, I believe will be soon. What I do know is that it could not have happened until all the pieces were in place. The pieces are now all in place except for Egypt and Iraq. It could happen in the next year or two. I believe that very soon after this takes place, we will see Revelation Chapter 17 fulfilled.

In Revelation Chapter 17, the Apostle John sees in a vision of a woman riding upon a scarlet beast with seven heads and 10 horns. The Bible refers to the church as the bride of Christ. This woman, however, is a very evil woman; she is called the great harlot or prostitute. She has clothes of purple and scarlet. Her jewelry is of precious stones and pearls. In her hand is a golden cup filled with filth and abominations. On her forehead a name was written, "Mystery, Babylon the Great, the Mother of Harlots and of the abominations of the earth." She is described as being drunk with the blood of the saints and of the martyrs of Jesus. Many people believe that this is the picture of an apostate, false church which persecutes the true church. Historically from the time of the Reformation many people have identified this false church with the Papacy of the Roman Catholic Church.

It has been estimated that the popes of Rome tortured and killed 50 or 60 million Christians over a period of several centuries simply because they would not submit to his authority. More recently, some people are saying that the coming Antichrist will be the Islamic Mahdi. This is certainly possible. Islam as a religion is antichrist. Mohammed and all of his followers are as antichrist as anyone could be and certainly the Mahdi fits the description of the antichrist. Whether the final antichrist is the Pope or the Islamic Mahdi, they are both the tools of Satan.

The woman is sitting on a scarlet colored beast with blasphemous names written all over it. It had seven heads and 10 horns. It bore a striking resemblance to the great red Dragon (Satan) in Revelation Chapter 12:1.

In Revelation 17:9, we are told that the seven heads are seven mountains on which the woman sits. The city of

Rome is built upon seven mountains. These seven heads also represents seven Kings or Kingdoms. In verse 10 we read that five Kings or Kingdoms have already fallen, one is and the other has not yet come.

At the time the apostle John is writing these words, the Western world was being ruled by the Roman Empire. Five world empires had already fallen, they are: the Egyptian, the Assyrian, the Babylonian, the Persian, and the Macedonian Greek Empire.

In verse 10 we read that one is (the Roman Empire), and the other has not yet come, and when he comes he must continue a short time. The Roman Empire broke up in three sections. The western part of the Roman Empire fell to the barbarians in 476 A.D., the Middle East and Africa fell to Islam in the seventh century, and in 1453 A.D. Constantinople (the capital of the eastern Roman Empire) was conquered by Islam.

After the Western Empire fell, it wasn't long before the papacy co-opted the Gothic Kings and then established the Holy Roman Empire. We believe the Holy Roman Empire to be the seventh King or kingdom.

In verse 11 we read, "The beast that was, and is not, is himself also the eighth, and is of the seven, and is going to perdition." Here we see the beast that was (The Holy Roman Empire) came to an end during the time of the Reformation. Napoleon tried to resurrect the world empire, but he failed. Hitler also tried to set up the Third Reich, (the third incarnation of the Roman Empire) but he also failed. In this passage however, we see that there will be another world empire, although it is destined to last only a very short time.

The eighth kingdom is the New World Order. It is of the seven. It takes on the characteristics of the first seven empires, but it will only last for a very short time.

In verses 12 & 13, we read, "The 10 horns which you saw are 10 Kings who have received no kingdom as yet, but they shall receive authority for one hour as Kings with the beast. These are of one mind, and they will give their power and authority to the beast."

Many people have thought that these 10 Kings are various nations of the European Common Market. However, the European Common Market has never been made up of 10 nations for any length of time. There is, however, a better explanation. The United Nations has divided the whole world into 10 administrative zones. One of the zones is the North American zone. This zone includes Mexico, the United States and Canada. Knowing this helps to explain some of the things that have been happening regarding illegal immigration and the plans to build a super highway and rail system from Mexico through the United States and into Canada.

We read that these 10 Kings or kingdoms will reign one hour with the beast. A prophetic day usually stands for one year. If that is the standard to be used one hour would be about two weeks. However that is long enough. Time is a relative thing. If you're having a good time an hour doesn't seem very long, but if you were sitting on a hot stove one minute would seem like an eternity. This chapter in the book of Revelation is immediately followed with judgment and the return of the Lord Jesus Christ.

CHAPTER 22

THE FINALE

HOW MUCH TIME DO WE HAVE?

I don't know, it's impossible to say. The invasion of Israel could happen very soon. By the time you read these words, it may have already happened. The fulfillment of Revelation chapter 17 may take a little longer. I believe there will probably be at least a year or two after Israel is invaded before the powers that be feel it is the right time to make that final push to establish the New World Order.

WHAT SHOULD WE DO NOW?

America must return to its Godly roots, the Declaration of Independence, the Bill of Rights, and the Constitution of the United States if it is to continue to be the land of the free and the home of the brave.

The Bible says,

> "If my people, which are called by my name, shall humble themselves, and pray, and seek my face, and turn from their wicked ways; then will I hear from heaven, and will forgive their sin, and will heal their land." 2 Ch 7:14

Notice that this scripture does not say that the whole nation has to humble itself, pray and repent. Instead, God calls upon the people called by His Name, the Christians, to humble themselves, pray and turn from their wicked ways. If God's people call upon Him, He will hear from heaven, forgive their sin, and heal their land.

WILL GOD'S PEOPLE HUMBLE THEMSELVES, PRAY AND REPENT?

I don't know, but I certainly hope so. America is at the tipping point. If America comes to its senses and pulls back from the brink, it would still be possible for it to return to its historical and spiritual roots; but if it continues much longer in the direction it is going, it will plunge down headfirst into the abyss.

REASONS WHY GOD'S PEOPLE MIGHT NOT HUMBLE THEMSELVES, PRAY, AND REPENT.

Reason Number One: They don't recognize the danger because they don't understand what is happening.

Satan and his ruling elite have planned it that way. Early in the 20th century they took over the news media, used propaganda, and co-opted the educational system.

History has been rewritten in such a way that people have forgotten the reasons for the founding of this country and their godly heritage. The result is that after several generations, many people have no understanding of what has made our country great.

They do not realize that this country was founded as a republic, not a democracy, for a very good reason. The reason being, that all democracies in history have ended up in anarchy and then in despotism.

They do not understand the Godly heritage which was the foundation of this nation and our Constitution. They believe the lie that the Constitution of the United States calls for the separation of church and state. The First Amendment of the Constitution says something far different from that. The doctrine of separation of church and state was invented by a very liberal Supreme Court which used a letter of Thomas Jefferson as an excuse for their interpretation. In his letter though, Thomas Jefferson actually said just the opposite of their interpretation

OUR RESPONSE:

Jesus said the truth will set you free. The truth is available but you have to look for it. One of the purposes of this book is to sound the alarm to wake people up.

Reason Number Two: They are so concerned about what they think is good for them that they overlook what might be good for the country, the kingdom of God, and their children.

Almost everyone likes things that are free. When the government starts handing out free lunches, unemployment checks, guaranteed loans and so forth, the natural response is, "I'm a citizen, and I pay taxes, why shouldn't I accept it?"

Unfortunately these freebies are not free. Someone has to pay for them. Each freebie also comes with various laws and regulations which results in a loss of freedom. What is even worse is that people begin to think of government as big daddy.

To pay for all the freebies, people are taxed more and more. Therefore, they are unable to save for a rainy day and become more and more reliant upon the government for their very survival. The government which they thought was going to help them has now become their master and they have become slaves. At this point, many people want to elect public officials who will give them what they want, rather than what is good for the nation and for their children and grandchildren.

OUR RESPONSE:

It is unreasonable to expect people that are hungry to refuse a free lunch or for people who don't have a job to refuse unemployment compensation. It is also not reasonable to expect old people who have been robbed of their savings and self-reliance through taxes and inflation not to accept Social Security benefits. They believe they are owed these things **and they are**. Once social welfare programs have taken over more and more of the economy, it is impossible to stop them abruptly, but their expansion can be stopped. First, though, people need to come to understand the value of freedom, liberty, the ownership of property, and the opportunity of free enterprise and self-determination. Secondly, people need to turn away from the politics of envy and greed. Only then will they be willing to elect public officials who will do what is good for the country.

Reason Number Three: They have an escape mentality.

Many Christians who go to church every Sunday realize that bad things are happening in our country and in the world. They realize that morality in the United States is deteriorating. They can see the results of pornography, homosexuality, broken marriages, disobedient children, greed and violence. They also realize that plans are being made in our country and throughout the world to have a one world government, one world money system, and a universal one world religion.

So, what is the result? They sit back and say, "Praise the Lord! That means we're going to be ruptured soon." That is exactly the same thing that Chinese Christians did before and during World War II. Before the war Christian missionaries had gone to China and taught them about the coming Rapture of the Church. When the Chinese Communists took over they were slaughtered or put into slave labor camps. What was left of the church had to go underground. They were totally unprepared for what was coming.

Of course I believe that when the last trumpet blows Christians will be caught up to meet Christ in the air, but it is my contention that the teaching of a pre-tribulation rapture of the Church is based upon an incorrect understanding of the Scriptures. But even if that teaching is correct, are Christians supposed to simply sit back and wait for the Rapture?

WHAT DOES THE BIBLE SAY?

In Luke 19: 11-27, Jesus told the parable of the pounds. Jesus said that a nobleman was going away to receive his kingdom, but before he went, *"he called his ten servants, and delivered them ten pounds, and said unto them, Occupy till I come." Luke 19:13.*

He gave to each of his servants a pound for them to use while he was gone. Each pound represented a large sum of money which these servants were to use for their master's benefit. When the nobleman returned, he asked them what they had done with the pounds which he had given them to use. Most of the servants had used their pounds to invest and trade and had multiplied them. Their master then commended and rewarded them. One servant, however, said that he was afraid to trade and invest the pound, so he decided to keep it safe, wrapped in a napkin. The master was very angry. He said he could have at least put it in the bank to draw interest. So the master took the pound back and gave it to the one who had made the most money on his trading.

Jesus has also departed for a season and we are waiting for his return. Before he left, however, he earned great treasure for us. The treasure he has left us is far greater than gold or silver, diamonds or rubies, or all the money in the world.

1. He conquered temptation for us. (Luke 4:1-13). Jesus was perfectly obedient to his Heavenly Father and fulfilled all righteousness for us.

2. He paid our debt of Sin.

For he hath made him to be sin for us, who knew no sin; that we might be made the righteousness of God in him. (2 Co 5:21)

But if we walk in the light, as he is in the light, we have fellowship one with another, and the blood of Jesus Christ his Son cleanses us from all sin. (1 John 1:7)

Much more then, being now justified by his blood, we shall be saved from wrath through him. (Rom. 5:9)

Forasmuch as ye know that ye were not redeemed with corruptible things, as silver and gold . . . 19 But with the precious blood of Christ, as of a lamb without blemish and without spot: (1Peter 1:18,19)

3. He conquered death for us.

Verily, verily, I say unto you, The hour is coming, and now is, when the dead shall hear the voice of the Son of God: and they that hear shall live. (John 5:25)

Jesus said unto her, I am the resurrection, and the life: he that believeth in me, though he were dead, yet shall he live: (John 11:25)

Yet a little while, and the world seeth me no more; but ye see me: because I live, ye shall live also. (John 14:19)

4. He conquered the devil for us.

For this purpose the Son of God was manifested, that he might destroy the works of the devil. (1John 3:8)

Be sober, be vigilant; because your adversary the devil, as a roaring lion, walks about, seeking whom he may devour: (1Peter 5:8)

Submit yourselves therefore to God. Resist the devil, and he will flee from you. (James 4:7)

Since Jesus has placed in our hands such great treasure to be used for his glory until he returns, should we not do everything possible to advance his kingdom? Absolutely! On this all Christians would agree. So far, though, I have only listed spiritual and eternal blessings. But, is that the only blessings and great treasure that Jesus has provided for us? Do we not live in a virtual promised land like God gave to Israel, a land flowing with milk and honey?

All citizens of the United States of America, (the greatest country on earth), have the blessings of life, liberty, and the pursuit of happiness as declared by the Declaration of Independence. These rights the Declaration says are not rights given by the government but are inalienable rights given by God, our Creator. This great treasure is not something we have earned, but it is something we have inherited from our forefathers and by the providence of Almighty God.

If then, we are thankful to Almighty God for providing us these blessings, and we are grateful to our forefathers who shed their blood that we might be free, and if we have any regard for the kind of land our children and grandchildren might have to live in, how then can we just sit back and do nothing?

A WORD OF WARNING!

God's judgment is coming to America because America has not repented. They have ignored the warning of 9/11; they have continued to kill and sell baby parts; they have embraced homosexuality and have made a mockery of marriage which God ordained; and through Obama America has turned against Israel. You can be absolutely sure of this, "God's judgment will come to America." As I write these words, the stock market fell about 600 points last week and 588 more points today. What else might happen I don't know but I believe this is just the beginning of the judgments God is going to pour out upon this nation.

WHAT CAN WE DO?

1. Heed the admonition found in **2 Chronicles 7:14 "If my people, which are called by my name, shall humble themselves, and pray, and seek my face, and turn from their wicked ways; then will I hear from heaven, and will forgive their sin, and will heal their land."** With God all things are possible. We are limited in what we can do, but He isn't.

2. Study to learn the truth and speak it to others. There are a number of books which will help you understand what the founding of this country was all about. The liberty and freedoms which we have inherited in this country cannot be taken for granted. There are those who want to take them away. Like

our forefathers, we must be willing to fight for them or they will disappear.

3. Don't be intimidated. Unless you are politically correct you will be persecuted. There are many groups today who use intimidation to shut up any kind of speech that does not agree with them. We must be willing to stand up and be counted.

4. Pastors, preach the WORD. Do not be intimidated by the IRS. Be willing, if necessary, to fight it out in court and to go to the aid of others who have to fight it out in court. Do not give in, even if it means giving up your non-profit status.

5. Be sure the ones you support for political office line up with God's Word. This is even more important than their speaking ability, their experience, qualifications, electability or the economy. Most likely, though, the one who lines up with God's Word will also be the best for the country and the economy.

6. Keep praying and seeking the Lord for wisdom. These are treacherous times. Your very life and the lives of your loved ones depend upon it.

One other thing, remember this!

Our God reigns

He is able to provide for us.

He is able to protect us.

Jesus won the victory for us.

Let us rejoice and be glad in him.

BIBLIOGRAPHY
(Recommended Reading)

Idols in the House by Ted Flynn,
        Published by MaxKul Communications Inc.,
        2002
Hope of the Wicked by Ted Flynn
        Published by MaxKul Communications Inc.,
        2000
Foreshocks of Antichrist by William T James (General
Editor)
        Harvest House Publishers, Eugene, OR 97402
Plucking the Eagle's Wings by Perry Stone
        Published by Voice of Evangelism 2001
        Cleveland, TN
Brotherhood of Darkness by Dr. Stanley Monteith
        Hearthstone Publishing, Oklahoma City,
        Oklahoma
Taking America Back by Joseph Farah
        WND Books (a division of Thomas Nelson, Inc.)
The Last Days in America by Bob Fraley
        Christian Life Services, Phoenix, AZ 85028
One World by Tal Brooke
        End Run Publishing, Berkeley, California
When the World Will Be As One by Tal Brooke
        Harvest House Publishers, Eugene, Oregon
The Demonic Roots of Globalism by Gary H. Kah

Huntington House Publishers, Lafayette,
Louisiana
Whatever Happened to the American Dream by Larry
Burkett
Moody press, Chicago, Illinois , 1993
The New World Order, by Pat Robertson
Word Publishing, 1991
The New Millennium, by Pat Robertson
Word Publishing, 1990

Highly recommended
http://www.wallbuilders.com/
http://www.wnd.com/
http://www.newsmax.com
Fox News

www.ingramcontent.com/pod-product-compliance
Lightning Source LLC
Chambersburg PA
CBHW022349280326
41935CB00007B/132